Nature Crafts Workshop

by Will Kirkman

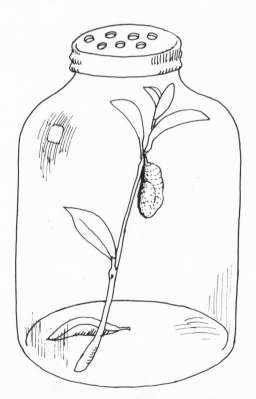

Fearon Teacher Aids, a division of PITMAN LEARNING, INC. Belmont, California

OTHER TITLES IN THE CRAFTS WORKSHOP SERIES:

INVENTORS WORKSHOP
MAKE YOUR OWN GAMES WORKSHOP
NATIVE AMERICAN CRAFTS WORKSHOP
TRASH ARTISTS WORKSHOP

Editorial director: Roberta Suid
Editor: Bonnie Bernstein
Production editor: Mary McClellan
Design manager: Eleanor Mennick
Designer and illustrator: Jane Mitchell
Cover designer: William Nagel

ISBN-0-8224-9781-6
Library of Congress Card Catalog Number: 80-84186
Printed in the United States of America.

1.9 8 7 6 5 4 3 2 1

Preface

Nature Crafts Workshop is a collection of more than 40 study and handicraft projects that draw on nature for their content and materials. The projects span many of the natural sciences: biology, botany, entomology, ornithology, zoology, and ecology. Each project is self-contained and fun, and each one yields a tangible item that kids can hang on the wall, give as a gift, or examine and study.

Whether the projects become part of the classroom nature and science program or provide a worthwhile opportunity for children and parents to work together on an activity of substance and interest, they should be a catalyst for more serious study. Although each project can be regarded as a means to fill a lag in a lesson plan, a long weekend, a summer day, or a rainy vacation, teachers and parents will find many ways to extend the project so that it serves a broader and more valuable education purpose.

Project directions are written so that kids at the intermediate and junior high level can work independently or with a minimum of adult guidance and supervision. Teachers and other adult participants can supplement each project with thoughtful questions and discussion. It is their job to stimulate and channel kids' interest and curiosity into further study and exploration. Questions invariably arise from kids themselves. While teachers and parents may not always have ready answers, they will want to have resources available so that kids can continue the exploration process. The Resources listed on page 80 provide classification and other information. It is just as important, however, to encourage kids to formulate their own questions and hypotheses. Through observation and the scientific method, kids can come up with their own solutions and theories.

Project materials are, for the most part, inexpensive or free— organic collectibles, leftovers, throwaways, and so forth. Individual projects become more instructive, however, when equipment such as a magnifying glass or a microscope is available. As materials are collected, participants young and old should ask all kinds of questions: Why does this flower bloom in spring and that one in summer? Why is this leaf green and that one red? Why is a caterpillar so different from a butterfly? Why are there so many shapes and colors among the seeds?·Why is bamboo hollow?

Curiosity is the one "material" that's needed in large supply. Don't follow each project prescriptively. If an activity involves gluing lentils and sunflower seeds to a frame, put a few in damp cotton to see what grows. Munch on others to see how they taste. Plant some seeds outdoors to replenish your seed supply for next year. A bag of seeds from the grocery store will satisfy all the demands of a project, but a whole dried sunflower full of seeds from last year's garden is much more wondrous and revealing.

Nature Crafts Workshop has six chapters—three on plants and plant materials and three on animals. The first chapter involves crafting plant materials gathered from a garden or a field. Field notes and resource findings enhance the finished item—nature preserved as art or used for scientific display. Either way, a little collecting can teach a lot of botany.

Chapter Two uses seeds, fruits, and dried materials as the media for works of art and gifts such as musical instruments as old as humankind—panpipes and reed hummers. Most of the materials are collectible or growable, the latter requiring only a corner of a schoolyard, a small garden, or a window box at home.

Chapter Three involves growing plants. Most of these projects require little more than a container of water, a window ledge, and sunlight. Activities range from forcing bulbs to bloom in a dish and growing large pumpkins with names in their skins to building your own greenhouse.

Chapter Four explores the differences between species of animals, specifically insects and arachnids. Projects involve keeping, breeding, and observing small creatures in order to learn about their habits and habitats. Nature crafts in this chapter can be regarded as the techniques for caring for and studying bugs and organisms.

Chapter Five features bird and bird-watching projects. Lightweight construction is involved in making several bird feeders and houses. In the city or the country, in a house or apartment, or in a schoolyard or backyard, birds are a fascinating subject for observation and crafts activities.

Chapter Six involves the more extended care, breeding, and observation of larger animals. Most projects require the construction and careful design of an appropriate habitat in which kids can nurture a particular animal or family of animals, such as chicks, fish, or a variety of amphibians.

In addition to the Resources, **Nature Crafts Workshop** includes a section of Field Charts and Diagrams that may be duplicated for individual or classroom use. These illustrated pages and note-keeping records will be handy for much of the fieldwork featured in this book. They are conveniently cross-referenced to appropriate **Workshop** projects.

Whether a project involves the crafting of an attractive work of art from natural materials or the care of animals in replicas of their natural environments, kids and adults alike should learn to regard nature with appreciation and respect. A seed mosaic carefully executed is certainly lovely, but the seeds themselves are interesting and beautiful in their own right. Captive animals have the right not only to good care but also to a safe return to their original environments once they have served as tools for learning.

Nature is interesting, usable, worthy of respect, and accessible. **Nature Crafts Workshop** is written to help kids and adults discover that it's not necessary to relegate nature to somewhere out there beyond the freeway. It's possible to pick a weed in a vacant lot or lift a cobweb in an attic to find a whole world of life opening up between your hands.

Contents

Plant Specimens

The projects in Chapter One cater to the assumption that everyone likes to collect things. These collection and craft activities are designed to make the most of this natural tendency. They show how even a handful of wilted dandelions can become a permanent and beautiful wall decoration; or part of a young botanist's herbal; or the raw materials for a one-of-a-kind T-shirt, gift wrap, Christmas gift, or birthday present.

The techniques for collecting and crafting are easy and will require only a minimum of adult supervision. School-aged kids can manage the picking, pressing, and mounting activities on their own. Parents and teachers can help by gathering other necessary materials and resources, such as a good wild flower or garden flower identification book, and by providing lots of opportunities for taking collecting jaunts.

Pressed Flowers and Plants

There are dozens of ways to preserve flowers and leaves to create a permanent collection. The easiest method by far is pressing and drying the plant materials between layers of blotting paper or newspaper. This first activity describes the procedure for pressing plant parts; the next four projects provide instructions for using pressed materials in works of art.

The pressing of flowers must be preceded by an excursion to collect them. The Field Notes on Collecting Plants, page 4, offer some tips on collecting. One thing to keep in mind is that pressing plants will be a far more interesting and valuable experience if you know what you've got. Collectors should take along notebooks to record the month, the day, the location, and the name of each specimen. There are three pages in the section of Field Charts and Diagrams at the back of this book that will be useful: the Diagram of Flowers, page 83; the Diagram of Leaf Prints, page 84; and the form for taking Plant Collecting Notes, page 85. A wild flower manual or garden book is helpful for identifying most unfamiliar plants (see Resources, page 80).

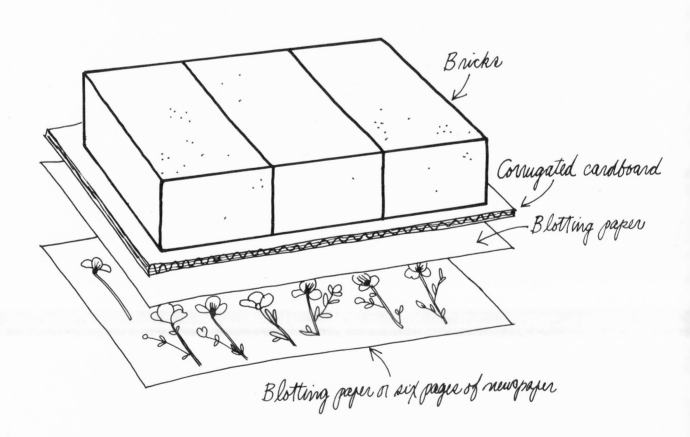

Bricks

Corrugated cardboard

Blotting paper

Blotting paper or six pages of newspaper

YOU WILL NEED

Newspaper or blotting paper (several sheets)
Flowers with stems and leaves attached or leaves from trees or
   bushes (see the Field Notes on Collecting Plants, page 4)
Large piece of corrugated cardboard (cut from a box)
Heavy objects such as large books or bricks

HERE'S WHAT TO DO

1. Choose a table or a part of the floor on which you can leave
   your flowers for a week or so without having to move them.
   Place a piece of blotting paper or a section of newspaper six
   pages thick on the flat surface.
2. Put a few flowers or leaves on the paper; they should all be
   of about the same thickness. Arrange them so that they don't
   touch and so that no parts will fold over when you cover
   them up.
3. Carefully put a second piece of blotting paper or section of
   newspaper on top. On top of that put a piece of corrugated
   cardboard large enough to cover all the flowers and leaves.
   (If your blotting paper or corrugated cardboard isn't very
   large, you can press the flowers in two or three layers. Lay
   down the first piece of paper, then some flowers, then more
   paper, then more flowers. Don't make a "sandwich" more
   than three flower layers thick, though.)
4. Press down on the cardboard to flatten the flowers. Place
   several heavy books, bricks, or other heavy objects on top so
   that the weight evenly presses down on the cardboard. Don't
   forget the edges.
5. Wait at least three to four days, maybe a week or more. If
   you want to check the drying process, take off the weights
   and lift up one corner. When the flowers are ready, they will
   be stiff and very dry. Thick flowers take longer.
6. When the flowers are dried, very carefully put them into a
   box. (A shoe box or a shirt box is fine.) They break easily, so
   don't bend or squash them. Keep them in the box until you're
   ready to use them in one of the projects that follow.

Flatten the large flower heads. Spread the petals evenly.

Press grasses in natural curves.

Store dried flowers in a shoe or shirt box

COLLECTING PLANTS

A haphazard collection of plant materials may result in a dull potpourri of plant parts. A jaunt with a plan and a purpose, however, can yield an attractive and well-organized collection. For instance, in one jaunt search for specimens of a certain genus of plants; in another, take samples of all the wild flowers growing in a defined area.

Collectors in urban areas may find that the easiest plants to collect are those that most people call weeds: dandelion, wild mustard, wild radish, and shepherd's purse. Suburban collectors may have gardens in their own yards or on the school grounds. People who live in the country or who go there often can gather both weeds and wild flowers.

A good plan for collecting plant specimens in the city is to go to the same group of trees and bushes in a park in early fall, late fall, early spring, and late spring or summer. During each visit, take a leaf from each plant and record the date, the weather conditions, and the name of the plant. If the plant produces seeds or flowers at certain seasons, take specimens of each of these as well. For example, a maple tree will have large green leaves in early fall, colored leaves in late fall, then soft and fragile leaves in spring. In spring the tree will also flower. Later on it will seed, releasing interesting winged pods. Specimens from the maple tree should be dried and then mounted on a single album page (see An Herbal in an Album, page 5). Write the plant name at the top of the page. Then from field notes copy the collection dates under the various leaves, flowers, and seed specimens. The page now represents a picture of the entire life-cycle of the maple tree. Additional notes on weather may give some clues to why the changes take place.

Use similar methods of collecting, recording, and mounting flowers and plants from gardens, fields, or vacant lots. A finished display of a year's growth will reveal a lot about how plants reflect the seasons and how they adapt to environmental conditions.

An Herbal in an Album

An herbal is a permanent collection of dried plant parts with notes on what each specimen is and where it came from. An herbal is more useful and interesting to a botanist if there is a limit to what's in it. For instance, an herbal might contain only spring-blooming flowers or only leaves and flowers from the trees of one neighborhood or one region. Even if the herbal is a miscellaneous collection, individual pages of the album should feature material from a single plant. Each page should include field notes—some scientific information and some personal observations. Here's a sample entry:

> *Escholtzia californica* (California poppy).
> May 24, full sun. Found growing in sunny meadow near oaks and madrones. Also in bloom: lupine, checkerbloom, and yarrow.

Acetate sleeve

CALIFORNIA POPPY

WILD ONION

Punch your own holes in sheets of construction paper. Use a three-ring binder.

YOU WILL NEED

Mounting paper (see note following directions for suggestions)
Pressed, dried plant parts (see Pressed Flowers and Plants, page 2)
Stick glue (from grocery or stationery store)
Felt-tipped pen
Gummed labels (optional)

HERE'S WHAT TO DO

1. On a good work surface—a work table in the classroom, a dining room table, or a big desk—set out your materials. Place a single piece of mounting paper in front of you. Arrange one kind of plant material on it until you think it looks nice. Leave enough space to add your field notes. Look at the illustration for ideas.
2. When you are satisfied with the arrangement, lift up one piece of dried plant material and rub stick glue over the page underneath. Put the dried plant back and press down carefully. A block of wood makes a good presser. Do the same for the rest of the plant parts.
3. Neatly print the name of the plant at the top or bottom of the page with a felt-tipped pen; then copy in your field notes. If you don't wish to print right on the page, print on gummed labels (available at a stationery store) and stick them in the appropriate places. Or make your own paper labels and attach them with stick glue.

Note: You can mount your collection of plant materials on practically anything, depending on how you plan to display it. A few suggestions for inexpensive, ready-made albums appear in the illustrations.

A Framed Collection on the Wall

When a botanist wants a nuts-and-bolts collection, some kind of album is the answer. But those more artistically inclined can use pressed flowers to make striking wall displays. The flowers can be framed individually or clustered in small, identical frames. A framed collection might contain all the kinds of wild flowers from a single field or all the flowers that bloomed in one garden in spring. Small, inexpensive frames with glass or plastic to protect the display are available at variety stores. Keep framed collections out of strong light or the plant materials may fade to pale browns and creams.

YOU WILL NEED

Pressed, dried flowers with stems and leaves attached
Small, inexpensive frames made of plastic or wood and glass
Mounting paper such as bristol board or construction paper
Scissors
Stick glue
Field notes
Felt-tipped pen
Gummed labels (optional)
Matte board (optional)

HERE'S WHAT TO DO

1. Sort pressed, dried flowers into kinds. Each small frame will hold just one kind of flower, but you may want to include the seed pod or seed head as well as the flower. Or you may want to frame leaves taken from the same tree or bush in several seasons rather than flowering plants.
2. Take the frames apart carefully so as not to break the glass. Cut a piece of mounting paper that fits the backing of the frame exactly.
3. Arrange the flowers or leaves on the piece of mounting paper you have cut. When you like the arrangement, glue them to the paper with stick glue.
4. Add the name of the plant and field notes with a felt-tipped pen (or write the name and notes on a gummed label and stick it to the back of the frame when you finish).
5. Put the frame back together. If the plant parts are thick, you may want to matte them. This will help hold the glass away from the plants. You can cut your own matte or buy a ready-made border from an art supply or picture framing store.
6. Hang your whole display together and add to it as you collect more specimens. Try to maintain a theme, such as Our Garden, Leaves in All Seasons, or Schoolyard Wild Flowers.

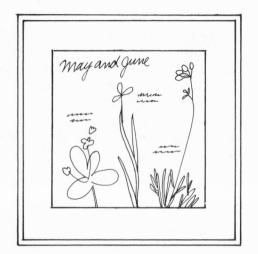

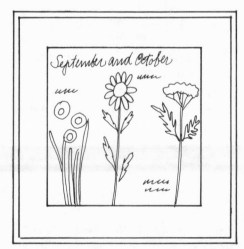

Flowers from the garden

Flowered Greeting Cards and Letter Paper

Small pressed flowers make delicate and original decorations for letter paper. Follow the instructions for pressing and drying on page 3, but choose tiny, simple flowers from weeds such as pimpernel, oxalis, and wild radish, and from cultivated plants such as violets and johnny-jump-ups. Flowers must not be used as decorations on the outside of envelopes unless letters are to be hand-delivered.

YOU WILL NEED

Small pressed flowers
Letter paper, cards, bristol board, or construction paper (without pattern)
Stick glue

HERE'S WHAT TO DO

1. Select one or two flowers for each piece of paper or individual card. If you can't find plain cards for sale, make them from bristol board or construction paper.
2. Arrange the flowers on the paper to see which position you like best—try a corner, the middle of the top, or the middle of the bottom.
3. When you've decided on the placement of the flowers, rub stick glue on the paper and press the flowers into position. Let the glue dry completely before you fold the paper to send it.
4. If you're making letter paper or note cards, make ten or more as a gift set. The set might include flowers of one kind or from one field or garden. Research the folklore of individual flowers to see which ones have attributes that are appropriate for the person you're giving the set to. Include that information on a little card with the gift.

Dried Bouquets

It's possible to dry many kinds of plant materials so that they keep their original shape. The dried materials can then be used in decorative, long-lasting bouquets.

Some plants dry very well on their own, while others require some sort of treatment. As a general guide, those plants that dry naturally when they grow only need to be collected and hung until they are dehydrated, while those that would naturally wilt need treatment.

There are three techniques for drying plant materials: the natural method, the glycerin method, and the silica gel method.

Natural Method

Toward the end of summer or at the beginning of autumn, some plants dry out and become stiff right where they grow. The sun, rain, and wind, however, may spoil their looks if you let them dry naturally. It's usually best to bring plants in for hanging when they are *almost* dry. There are two kinds of plants that will dry best indoors using the natural method. The first kind are grasses and other plants that usually grow wild. The second kind are garden flowers you may have to grow from seed.

YOU WILL NEED

Selection of the following plant materials:

Grasses and other wild plants: wheat, barley, rattlesnake grass, millet, timothy, buckwheat, teasel, milkweed pod, yarrow, and dock

Garden flowers: strawflower, everlasting, Chinese lantern, and moneywort

String

Scissors

Shady, sheltered place to hang plant materials

Vase or ribbon

HERE'S WHAT TO DO

1. Pick materials when they are already stiff. If you choose wheat or other grasses, pick long stems once they are no longer green.
2. Trim off any bits of leaf from the stems.
3. Tie the material in small bundles at the cut end of the stem. Leave a long tail of string so that you can use it to hang the bundle.

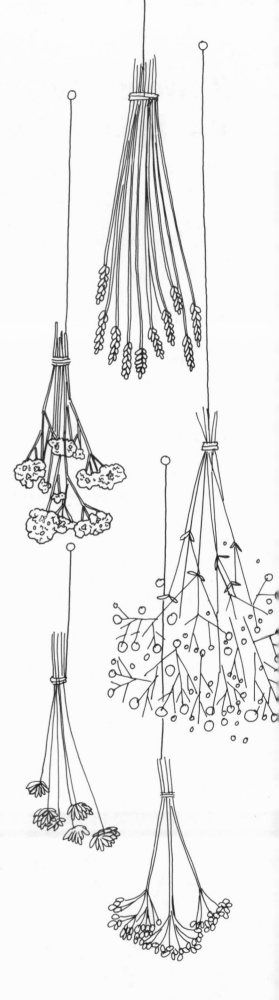

4. In a shady, sheltered place, hang the bundles so that they don't touch. Leave them until they are completely dry. If there's nothing to tie the strings to, hang the bundles from a piece of rope stretched between two walls.
5. When the plants are dry, arrange several kinds together in a vase or tie an assortment together with a ribbon for a gift. Remember, they break easily when dry.

Glycerin Method

Plants with very thick leaves or thick flowers dry better when treated with glycerin, which keeps them from becoming entirely hard and helps them hold their shape. However, the glycerin may change the color of the plant material.

YOU WILL NEED

Selection of plant material such as evergreen magnolia leaves and artichoke and thistle blooms
1 cup of glycerin (available at hobby shops or drugstores) in 1 gallon of water
Small bucket or large jar
Vase

HERE'S WHAT TO DO

1. Mix the glycerin and water in a small bucket or large jar. Stir well.
2. Cut branches, long-stemmed thistle or artichoke blooms, or other material, and strip away leaves at the cut end of the stem.
3. Put the cut end into the glycerin water, and let it stand a week or more. The plants will dry and may change color, but they will not be stiff and hard. When they're ready, they will be leathery.
4. Throw away the water, and arrange the plant material in a vase. The arrangement will last several years if it's dusted regularly.

Silica Gel Method

The silica gel method is good for drying soft flowering plants from a garden or field, such as many varieties of narcissus. It works best with simple flowers or flowers that have only one row of petals. A thick or double flower, such as the tuberous begonia, Shasta daisy, or double rose, does not dry well in silica gel.

Mix 1 cup glycerin with 1 gallon water.

YOU WILL NEED

Selection of the following flowers: single roses; violet; viola; pansy; narcissus, such as jonquil; lily; and daisy, such as marguerite and black-eyed susan
Silica gel (available at hobby shops)
Shoe box or other small carton
Vase or covered glass container

HERE'S WHAT TO DO

1. Pour silica gel into a shoe box or small carton to make a layer about one-half inch deep.
2. Lay a few flowers on the silica gel, making certain that they don't touch each other.
3. Pour in more silica gel. Cover the flowers slowly, and as you cover them, arrange them so that they keep their natural shapes. Don't squash them flat under the crystals.
4. Wait a week or more. Thick petals and double flowers may take longer.
5. Carefully push the silica gel aside and lift the flowers out. If they are not quite dry, bury them again.
6. When the flowers are dry, arrange them in a bouquet. They will last for years arranged in a covered glass container.

Pour in more silica gel.

½ inch silica gel

Decorated Candles

Partially dried and pressed flowers, leaves, and grasses of medium thickness are just right for this project. The candles, however, should be the large, heavy kind that are lit on holidays, although ordinary candlestick candles will work with thinner and more delicate dried plants. The project will be easier if the candles are not too tall.

Candles with flower and leaf designs make unusual, decorative centerpieces, mantle displays, colossal birthday candles, or holiday giveaways.

YOU WILL NEED

Partially dried and pressed flowers, leaves, or grasses (They should be flattened but still bendable.)
Stick glue
Candles
Coffee can
Paraffin wax, enough to fill the can

HERE'S WHAT TO DO

1. Dry the flowers for about two days (see Pressed Flowers and Plants, page 2). If they are too dry they will break when you try to fit them to the rounded candle.
2. Hold dried flowers or other plant parts against the side of the candle to see how they'll look. If you like the effect, rub glue on the candle and stick them on.
3. Let the glue dry for an hour or two.
4. Put a coffee can filled with paraffin wax into a pan partly filled with water. Heat the water so that the wax melts. Don't turn the heat up too high—just high enough so that the wax is slightly bubbling. You may have to add a bit more wax as it melts. The can should be about two-thirds full of melted wax when you're ready. If the can is too full of wax, the wax will overflow when the candle is dipped. If it's not full enough, the entire candle will not be covered.
5. Dip the decorated candle into the wax and take it out quickly. You only want a very thin coat of wax over your plant decoration.
6. Set the candle upright on a sheet of wax paper or in a candlestick until it is cool and hard. It's ready to give away or to keep for a personal decoration.

Note: Using the paraffin requires special care. Paraffin wax can catch fire and burn if you spill it.

Glue flowers onto candle. Dip into can of melted paraffin wax.

Can 2/3 full of wax

Dry on wax paper.

Mushroom Spore Prints

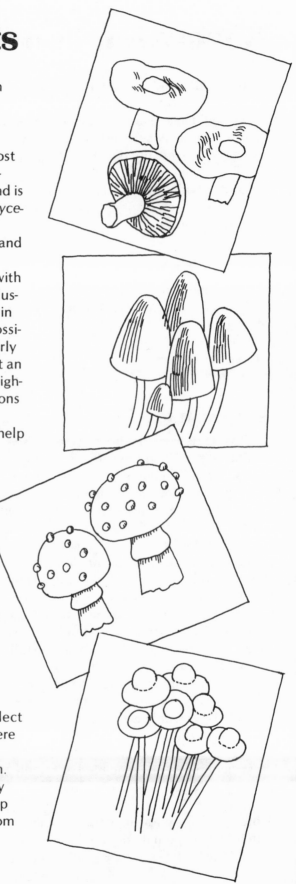

Most people think of a mushroom as a small white or brown fungus bought at a grocery store. Fungi that grow wild—toadstools—can be inedible, poisonous, or sometimes a bit frightening.

All of the fungus relatives are interesting. They grow almost anywhere—from the countryside to a vacant lot. The mushroom or toadstool or puffball that is visible above the ground is a kind of flower or fruit growing from the real plant—the *mycelium.* The mycelium is always hidden in the soil or in rotten wood or in other material that the fungus is breaking down and digesting.

The study of mushrooms and their relatives should start with a book or field guide that provides good descriptions and illustrations. Several are listed in Resources on page 80. Collect in spring or autumn, using a basket, a trowel, and a knife. If possible, take a camera with a lens that lets you take pictures fairly close to small objects. Photograph the mushrooms and start an album with pictures and descriptions of all the fungi in a neighborhood or region. The following two sets of project directions explain how to collect fungi and how to make spore prints. They also suggest how to make field observations that will help you identify the various kinds of fungi.

Collecting Fungi

YOU WILL NEED

Trowel or other small digging tool
Small, sharp knife
Basket
Book that identifies mushrooms
Camera that takes clear pictures from 3 feet (optional)

HERE'S WHAT TO DO

1. In spring or fall when the weather is rainy and warm, collect your equipment and look for mushrooms almost anywhere outdoors.
2. If you're using a camera, take a picture of the mushroom. Then with a trowel carefully dig and scrape the soil away from the stem. Some mushrooms grow from a kind of cup that is hidden in the ground, and if you pick the mushroom you won't see it.
3. Some mushrooms grow like shelves on the sides of tree trunks or posts. Use the knife to cut them.

4. Loosely arrange the mushrooms in the basket. They'll break easily if they tumble or are squashed.
5. Use a book to identify each mushroom in the collection. Then make spore prints.

Note: Field notes will help in identifying mushrooms that are described in a field guide book. Here are the kinds of observations that should be recorded:

What was nearby the mushroom? If the mushroom was found near a tree, identify the tree.

Did the mushroom stem grow from a cup in the ground?

Does the stem have a ring around it?

Turn the mushroom upside down. Are there slots or tubes underneath?

What color is the top? The stem?

Are there any spots or patches on the top?

Making Spore Prints

YOU WILL NEED

White paper or black paper
Small, sharp knife
Mushroom caps with stems cut off very close to the cap
Bowl or jar
Microscope (optional)

HERE'S WHAT TO DO

1. Put a sheet of white paper on a table where it can stay for several hours or overnight.
2. Carefully cut the stem of a mushroom near the cap, and put the cap on the paper with gills or tubes down.
3. Cover the mushroom by turning a bowl or jar upside down over it, and let it stay for at least two to three hours.
4. Lift off the bowl and pick up the mushroom without sliding it. On the paper you will see a kind of spiderweb of spores, sometimes dark-colored, sometimes pale.
5. Look at a few spores under a microscope, if you have one. Each kind of mushroom has spores of a different shape.
6. The color of the spores tells you what group of mushrooms yours belongs to. If you have a white-spored kind, you can see the pattern by getting down to the level of the paper and looking sideways across it or by making another print on black paper.

Cut stem near cap.

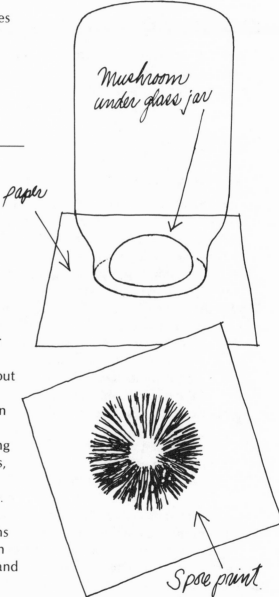

paper

Mushroom under glass jar

Spore print

Leaf Prints

Large and small leaves can be used with paints and inks for printing. Use just one kind of leaf or select several different leaves that are interesting together. Print on sheets of paper for gift wrap, on cloth for napkins, on handkerchiefs or tablecloths, or on plain T-shirts for one-of-a-kind clothing.

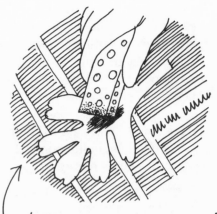

Work on top of newspapers when you put paint on the leaf.

YOU WILL NEED

Leaves (Choose undamaged leaves that will press flat easily.)
Paints or textile dyes (see Note for suggestions)
Newspaper
Saucer or waxed paper
Sponge
Paper or cloth (without pattern)
Paper towels
Roller (You can buy a special artist's or printer's brayer or just use an old rolling pin or a bottle.)
T-shirts
Cardboard

HERE'S WHAT TO DO

1. Spread out newspaper to cover your work area. Select the first leaf. Wash it if it's dusty and dry it completely. Be sure it will press flat when you use a roller on it.
2. Place a dab of paint in a saucer or on a square of waxed paper. Wet a small sponge and squeeze it as dry as possible, then dip it in the paint (you need only a little paint).
3. Dab the paint all over the upper, smooth side of the leaf so that it is evenly coated.
4. Place the leaf paint-side down on the cloth or paper. (Be careful not to slide it.) Cover it with a clean paper towel.
5. Roll over the paper towel slowly and evenly.
6. Lift off the paper towel and the leaf. You have your first print. Repeat the procedure for additional prints.

Note: If you want a whole sheet of repeated prints, always start on the part of the paper or cloth that is farthest away from you. That way you won't smudge the old prints as you make the new ones. Let the printed paper dry thoroughly before you use it. For T-shirts, put a piece of cardboard *inside* the shirt so that you won't print through to the next layer.

If you want to create a personal gift wrap for holiday or birthday gifts, choose among the many colors of acrylic paints available in an art supply store. Small tubes go a long way.

For cloth projects such as a set of napkins or a T-shirt, look for color-fast textile dyes in a hobby shop or art supply store.

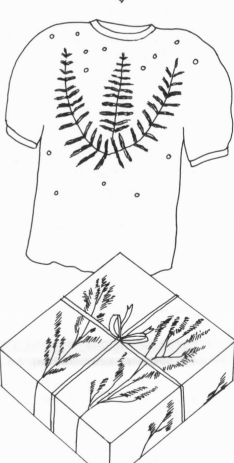

Seeds, Grasses, Fruits, and Gourds

Natural materials lend themselves to art and craft projects. There are so many interesting shapes and textures and such a variety of materials that simple techniques can turn natural materials into original works of art.

Some of the materials for projects in Chapter Two can be purchased at the grocery store. Other materials must be collected from gardens or the countryside, and *Lagenaria* gourds are hard to come by at all so you have to grow them yourself.

Whenever possible, kids should be included in gathering and preparing the materials. For example, a couple of Halloween pumpkins produce an abundance of seed for mosaics. Kids can help to clean and dry the seeds, and then toast a few for snacks.

Seed Mosaics

Seed mosaics are easy to make and can range from decorated drawings (a face, a horse) to complex and beautiful abstracts that take full advantage of the variety of seed shapes and colors. It is also possible to create a seed mosaic on the matte board border that decorates a mirror or picture inside a frame.

Seeds are readily available and very inexpensive, if not free for the finding. Beans, peas, and lentils of various sizes and colors are available at grocery stores. Pet shops and feed stores can supply sunflower seeds, corn, and various grains. A pumpkin or a large squash has an abundance of seeds that need only to be cleaned and dried. A garden may supply sweet peas, scarlet runner seeds, maple seeds, pine cone scales, or nasturtium seeds. In the fall, Indian corn and colored popcorn are available from florists and grocery stores.

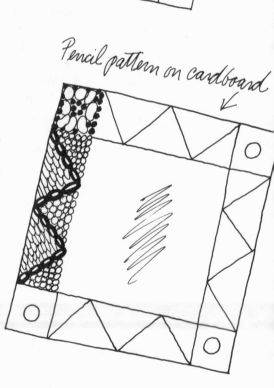

Glue seeds into position.

YOU WILL NEED

Corrugated cardboard
Matte knife or linoleum knife
Ruler and compass (optional)
Pencil
Seeds (various kinds)
White glue

HERE'S WHAT TO DO

1. Cut a small piece of corrugated cardboard in any shape you like. It takes a long time to cover a large area with seeds, so start fairly small. (To cut the cardboard, use a matte knife or linoleum knife and a ruler for straight edges.)
2. Pencil-sketch a picture on the cardboard or use a compass to make geometric designs. Keep the sketch simple. (If you are decorating a matte board border for a frame, sketch only the area that extends out beyond the frame.)
3. Choose the seeds you will use for the different parts of the mosaic. Remember that you will cover the whole piece of cardboard with seeds. Choose different seeds for the object of your sketch and for the background.
4. Begin near the middle. Put a small amount of white glue on the cardboard and lay a few seeds on it. Press down gently, then do some more. The mosaic will look nicer if you're careful to point all the seeds in the same direction.
5. Small round seeds such as millet make a nice background, since you can spread glue over a large part of the cardboard and sprinkle them on thickly. Let the glue dry completely and turn the mosaic over to remove the extra seeds.
6. Let the mosaic dry overnight. If any seeds come off, just dab on some glue and put them back.

Pencil pattern on cardboard

Acorn Jewels

Big seeds and nuts can be drilled and strung on cord or wire to make necklaces, brooches, and bracelets. The easiest seeds and nuts to find in most parts of the country are acorns and the big seeds of the buckeye or horse chestnut trees. You can also use edible chestnuts and such hard-shelled nuts as walnuts and pecans, but the hard shells make drilling more difficult. This project provides directions for making a necklace and a bracelet out of acorns.

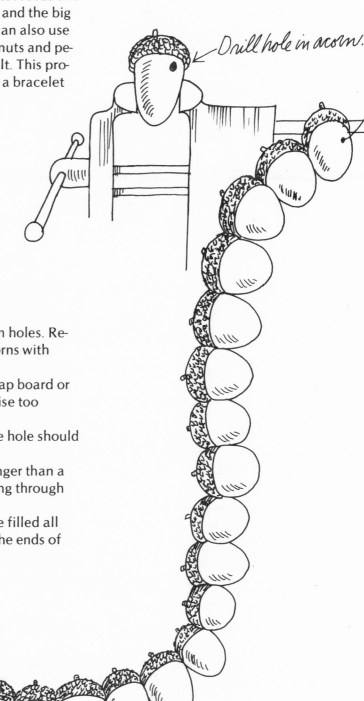

Drill hole in acorn.

YOU WILL NEED

Acorns
White glue
Clamp or small vise
Scrap board
Hand or electric drill and small drill bit
Kite string
Large needle

HERE'S WHAT TO DO

1. Sort the acorns and throw away those with worm holes. Remove the caps and glue them back onto the acorns with white glue to ensure that they won't fall off.
2. Clamp the acorns one at a time to a piece of scrap board or insert each in a vise. Don't screw the clamp or vise too tightly.
3. Drill a hole in each acorn near the wide end. The hole should be just big enough to insert a large needle.
4. Measure a piece of kite string about 3 inches longer than a necklace or bracelet. Thread one end of the string through the needle.
5. String the acorns close together. When you have filled all but about 1½ inches of string on each end, tie the ends of the string together.

Hand Puppets from Oak Galls

In many parts of the country, a small wasp lays its eggs in oak twigs, causing them to swell into large white galls. The outer covering of the gall is hard, but the inside is pithy and easy to cut.

If you know of a tree on which such galls grow, gather a few for finger puppets. Choose fresh ones at the end of spring when the wasp larvae have left. You'll know that the larvae have gone if there are small holes in the outer covering of the gall. These galls will be quite dry and easy to work with. Old galls from the ground may be discolored or spoiled.

Use acrylics to paint on the facial features and a scrap of cloth for a costume. Other decorations can be fashioned from natural materials. Use an acorn cap hat for example, or moss or lichen hair. The lichen called Spanish moss is especially good for this purpose.

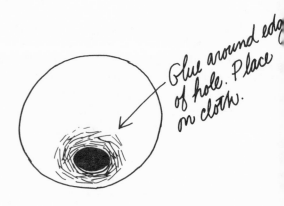

Glue around edge of hole. Place on cloth.

YOU WILL NEED

Large oak gall
Small, sharp knife
White glue
Scrap cloth for costume
Cardboard
Acrylic paints and small brush, or felt-tipped pens
Decorations (acorn cap hat, lichen hair)

Cloth

Cardboard

HERE'S WHAT TO DO

1. Gouge away a small area of the hard cover on a smooth side of the gall. Plan the cut so that the widest smooth area can be painted as a face. If the "stem" is interesting, plan to have it face forward as a nose.
2. Dig a hole into the pith just big enough to insert the first joint of a finger and tight enough so that the gall will stay on the finger. If you make the hole too big by accident, wind a piece of facial tissue around your finger before sticking it into the hole.
3. Dab a little white glue around the edges of the hole. Place a small square of cloth on a piece of cardboard, and set the gall in the center of the cloth. Hold it for a moment until it sticks. Let it dry overnight.
4. Once the glue has dried, slit the cloth so that your finger will go into the hole. Pull the rest of the cloth down around your finger as an outfit for the puppet.
5. Add facial features with acrylic paints or with felt-tipped pens. Add an acorn hat or some lichen hair.

Apple-Head Dolls

Apple-head dolls are easy to make. The basis is the apple head. This project features a simple stick body with a bandana outfit, but you can make the bodies as complicated as you like—sewing a wardrobe, adding arms, and so forth.

To dry the apple properly, keep it in a warm, dry place, or it will mold or spoil. The final result, with its soft wrinkles, looks exactly like an elderly person. You can add to the effect with paint and decorations by rouging the cheeks, reddening the lips, attaching a beard or mustache, and by using black or blue bead-headed pins or cloves for the eyes.

Each apple is a surprise. It isn't necessary to be exact with the initial carving of the facial features, since the carving will be exaggerated when the apple shrinks and dries.

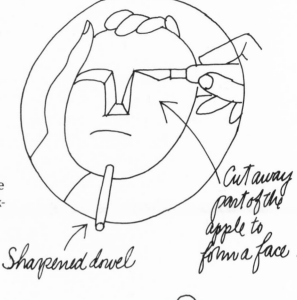

Cut away part of the apple to form a face.

Sharpened dowel

YOU WILL NEED

Firm apple such as Newtown Pippin or Rome Beauty (Delicious apples do not work as well.)
¼-inch dowel, about 1 foot long, sharpened at one end
Gouge or small knife
2 beaded pins or 2 cloves
Bottle (to stand doll in to dry)
Orange stick
Red paint
Cotton
Bandana
Ribbon
Scrap cloth for kerchief or hat

HERE'S WHAT TO DO

1. Peel the apple. At stem and flower end you may leave a tiny bit of peel. (See the Diagram of Fruits and Seeds on page 86 in the section of Field Charts and Diagrams.)
2. Insert the sharpened dowel through the flower end, about two-thirds of the way through the apple.
3. Using the knife or gouge, carve away a bit of apple to form the nose. You can also carve away a bit to form a chin.
4. Insert pins or cloves for eyes.
5. Stand the dowel in a bottle, and set the apple in a warm, dry place out of the sun. Let it dry completely (10–14 days).
6. When the apple is nearly dry, it's still pliable. Bring out the features by pressing around them with a blunt orange stick.
7. Once the apple is dry, add paint to rouge the cheeks and redden the lips. Cotton makes fine hair for the head and for extra facial features such as a beard or mustache.
8. Wrap the bandana around the dowel to form a costume, and tie it with a bit of ribbon. Tie on a kerchief or hat.

Reed or Willow Basketry

An attractive basket made from natural materials might serve as a pencil holder, a bread basket, a wastebasket, or a vase for a dried bouquet. A flatter version will make a plaque suitable for hanging.

Several natural materials lend themselves to basketry. Tall reeds work well, as do the long, flexible branches—the thinner the better—of weeping willow or weeping birch. Ordinary willow whips will do, but the ends may be too thick, which requires splitting them with a sharp matte knife. If natural materials are not available in sufficient quantities, hobby shops sell bundles of rattan. To this you can add a few natural branches.

A basic basket can be decorated with dried materials such as strawflowers or everlastings for a nice effect. Just weave soaked stems into the basketry.

YOU WILL NEED

Rattan (a 1-pound bag) or a large quantity of long, split reeds or
    flexible branches (willow, weeping willow, weeping birch)
    gathered in winter or early spring
Basin of warm water
Small amount of raffia or string

HERE'S WHAT TO DO

1. Select ten long strands of rattan or branches. The length determines the height of the finished basket. Soak the strands for an hour.
2. Follow the weaving pattern shown in the diagram to make the base. Lay five strands on a table parallel to each other. Lay five more across the middle at right angles to make a cross. These strands are the spokes.
3. Take another piece of rattan or branch to use as a weaver. Slide it under one group of five spokes. Weave it over the next five spokes, under the next five, and over the last five. Weave around the spokes like this four more times. Then trim the reed where you began to weave with it.
4. Separate the spokes into pairs. Weave over and under the pairs as shown in the diagram. Go all the way around once, keeping the pairs equidistant.
5. Now you need to add another spoke to make an odd number of spokes. If you continue with an even number, you'll be weaving under and over the same spokes each time around and the weaving will not hold together. Cut a strand of rattan or branch half the size of the original strands. Push it up through a hole in the base of the weaving as shown and trim it.

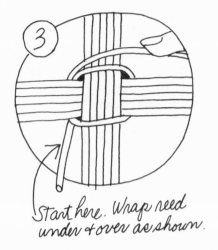

③ Start here. Wrap reed under + over as shown.

Continue weaving until completing 4 rounds. Then cut beginning reed.

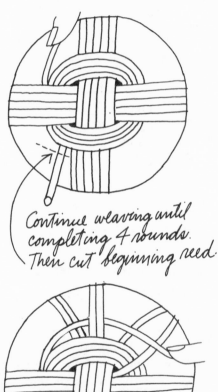

Separate the spokes into pairs. Weave over 2, under 2 for a complete round. Keep spokes equidistant.

6. Continue weaving under and over the spokes, treating the new single spoke like a pair.

7. If your reeds are short, tie several together with raffia to make long weavers. When a long weaver runs out, insert a new one by overlapping it with the end of the old one. Hold the ends together while you complete another round of weaving, then trim them so that each one rests against a pair of spokes and won't be noticed.

8. Weave flat until you have a base big enough for your basket. Weave one more round, but this time, separate the pairs of spokes and weave under and over each individual strand.

9. Gather the spokes upward and tie them loosely with a piece of raffia. Continue weaving between the individual spokes in a rising spiral. When your weaving holds the spokes upward by itself, snip off the raffia tie. Continue weaving, adding new weavers whenever necessary, until you have a basket that is the height you want.

10. Leave at least 4 inches of the spokes to finish off the basket. Bend these reed ends back over the last row of weaving, and weave them in and out down into the basket.

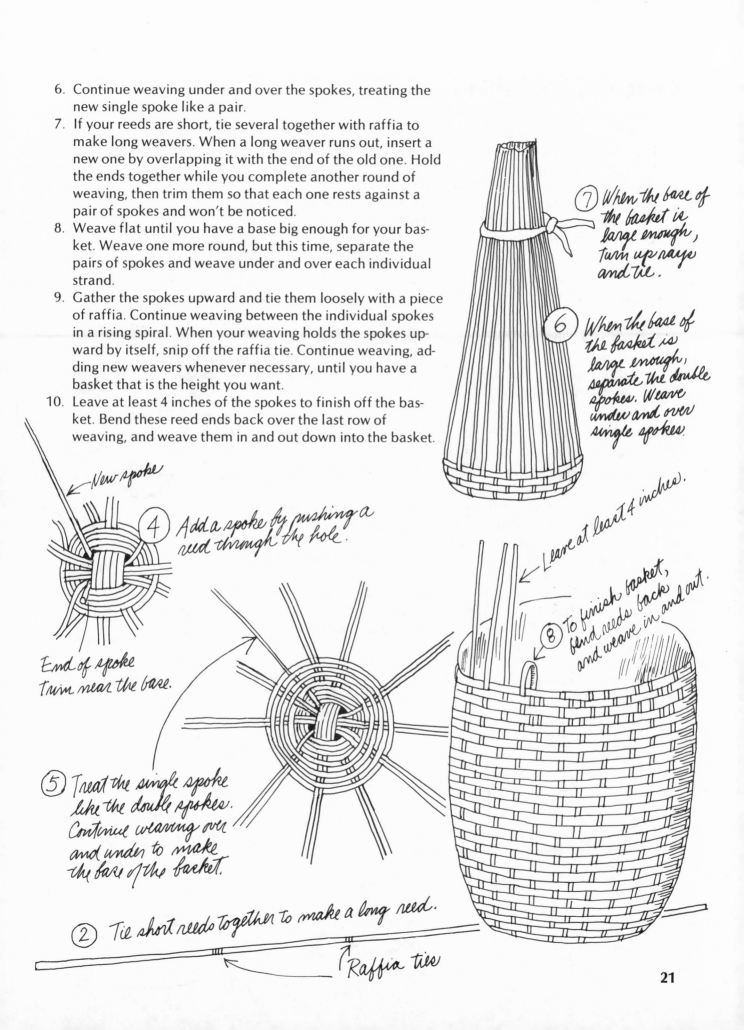

⑦ When the base of the basket is large enough, turn up rays and tie.

⑥ When the base of the basket is large enough, separate the double spokes. Weave under and over single spokes.

New spoke

④ Add a spoke by pushing a reed through the hole.

End of spoke Trim near the base.

← Leave at least 4 inches.

⑧ To finish basket, bend reeds back and weave in and out.

⑤ Treat the single spoke like the double spokes. Continue weaving over and under to make the base of the basket.

② Tie short reeds together to make a long reed.

Raffia ties

Gourd Hatrack

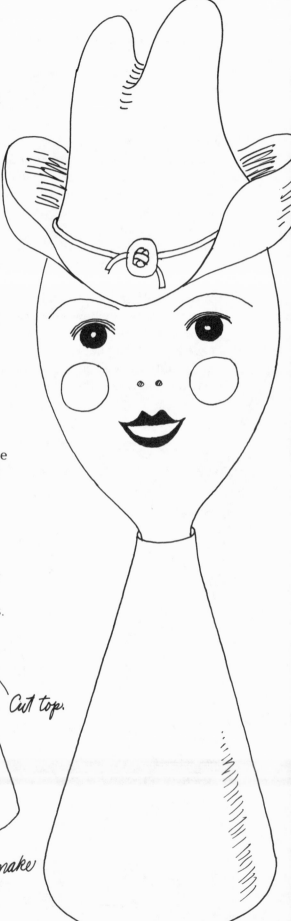

Lagenaria gourds are large white or beige gourds that become hollow as they dry. Occasionally, these gourds may be bought at florists and craft supply stores. Instructions for growing *Lagenaria* gourds are included in this book on page 32.

A large gourd makes a good kid's hatrack or costume wig stand. A cardboard cone supports it on a table. All in all, it looks rather dandy in a school props closet or on a dresser at home.

YOU WILL NEED

Large *Lagenaria* gourd (completely dry)
2' by 3' piece of light cardboard (preferably white)
String and pencil
Tape and glue
Paints or felt-tipped pens

HERE'S WHAT TO DO

1. Tie one end of a string about 2 feet long to the pencil.
2. Place the cardboard on a table and find the middle of one 3-foot side with a ruler. Mark it.
3. Hold the tip of the pencil at one end of the 3-foot side where you made the mark. Pull the string tight along the edge and hold it with your thumb on the mark.
4. Now swing the pencil across the cardboard to draw a half circle clear to the other edge.
5. Cut along the circle with scissors and overlap the edges to form a cone. Tape and glue the overlap and let it dry.
6. Cut away the tip of the cone just enough so that the narrow neck of the gourd will go in up to the round part.
7. Paint a face on the gourd, or draw one with felt-tipped pens. If you like, decorate the cone too.
8. Put a hat on the gourd.

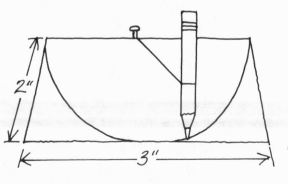

Cut top.

Overlay edge to make cone. Glue.

Gourds You Shake

Lagenaria gourds are naturally shaped and designed to make a rattle-type percussion instrument. Once the gourds are thoroughly dry, the seeds loosen inside. Shaking the gourds produces a sound like a muffled maraca. To increase the noise level, add a few pebbles through a tiny hole. Then wind a raffia braid around the gourd to block the hole and to form a colorful handle.

YOU WILL NEED

1 or 2 completely dry *Lagenaria* gourds
Hand or electric drill and ¼-inch drill bit
5 or 6 tiny pebbles or beads (less than ¼-inch in diameter)
Raffia (6 long strands)
Kraft paper
White glue
Large needle and thread

HERE'S WHAT TO DO

1. Choose a gourd with a round bottom and long slender neck. Shake the gourd hard several times. You should be able to hear the seeds rattle. If you don't, the gourd is not dry enough.
2. Drill a ¼-inch hole in the gourd where the round part begins to bulge away from the neck. Hold the gourd neck up and drill downward.
3. Push in the pebbles or beads and shake. Add more if you want to increase the sound.
4. Braid six strands of raffia in a tight, three-part braid. You'll need quite a long braid, 3 to 6 feet depending on the diameter of the gourd's neck (make more than you need and you can cut off the excess). Use two colors of raffia if you like.
5. Cut a small patch of kraft paper or other heavyweight paper about ½-inch on a side, and glue it over the hole in the gourd.
6. Glue down 2 inches of the end of the braid with the rest of the braid pointing away from the round part of the gourd.
7. When the end is stuck tight, rub white glue around the end of the neck (leave the tip uncovered), and wind the braid in a spiral up the handle so that it covers the end bit that you glued on (see the diagram).
8. Keep gluing and winding until you cover the paper patch. Then sew the end of the braid to the last row back. Rub white glue over the whole raffia part of the handle. Let the glue dry overnight. Shake your gourd.

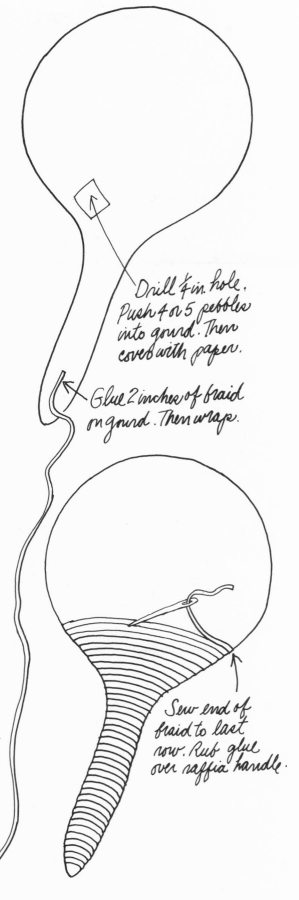

Drill ¼ in. hole. Push 4 or 5 pebbles into gourd. Then cover with paper.

Glue 2 inches of braid on gourd. Then wrap.

Sew end of braid to last row. Rub glue over raffia handle.

Reed or Bamboo Hummers

Almost everyone has played a comb covered with tissue paper. When you hum against the covered comb, the paper vibrates and adds to the humming.

Here is a simple instrument that copies the effect but is somewhat better looking. In France it's called a *mirliton*. We call it a hummer.

YOU WILL NEED

Large segment of bamboo or reed cut from between the joints
    to make a hollow tube
Sandpaper
Hand or electric drill and ¼-inch bit
Rat-tail file
Large onion
Basin of warm water
Small amount of raffia

HERE'S WHAT TO DO

1. Reed and bamboo grow in sections with a joint between each one. The reed is closed off inside at the joint. To make a hummer, you need to cut a large segment of bamboo from *between the joints* so that it is open at both ends. Sand the ends of the bamboo tube if they are rough.
2. Drill a ¼-inch hole in one side of the bamboo about one-third of the way from one end.
3. Using the rat-tail file, carefully enlarge the hole to a rectangle about ½-inch long.
4. Peel the dry skin from an onion, and soak it in the warm water until it is no longer brittle. Cover both ends of the bamboo tube with onion skin tied tightly with raffia.
5. Let the onion skin dry overnight. Now put your mouth over the hole and hum a song. The skin will vibrate and add music to your humming.

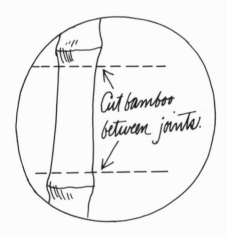

Cut bamboo between joints.

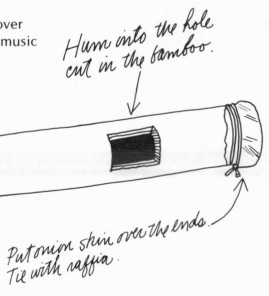

Hum into the hole cut in the bamboo.

Put onion skin over the ends. Tie with raffia.

Reed or Bamboo Panpipes

Panpipes are probably the oldest reed instruments. You can make them fairly easily if you have access to stiff reeds or small or medium-sized bamboo. The principle involved is exactly that of a flute, but you may be more familiar with the concept in terms of blowing over the neck of a soda bottle. When you blow *across* the open end (not *into* it), the column of air inside vibrates. You get a high note with a short tube or full bottle and a low note with a long tube or empty bottle. The diameter of the hole has an effect too—high for narrow, low for wide.

It's very difficult to tune simple pipes and make them quality instruments, although with patience, it can be done. Most people will nevertheless enjoy playing their pipes as a simple reed whistle even if the music is a bit cacophonous.

YOU WILL NEED

3 to 5 lengths of reed or bamboo, about 3-feet long and with an inside hole about 1/2-inch to 3/8-inch in diameter
Small saw
Sandpaper
Tongue depressors or split reed
Small amount of raffia

HERE'S WHAT TO DO

1. For the first pipe, cut a length of reed or bamboo just below a joint and again just below the next one. You will have a short tube with one end closed. Blow sharply across the open end and you will hear a whistle. Short tubes will make a higher whistle, long ones a lower whistle. One end always has to be at a joint so that it is shut.
2. Smooth off the open end with sandpaper.
3. Cut up to ten tubes, each about 1/2-inch shorter than the last, but make certain that one end is a closed joint. Sandpaper the open ends.
4. Sandwich the first tube between the ends of two tongue depressors or two pieces of split reed about 1 1/2 inches below the open end. Bind them together with raffia in a crossover pattern as shown in the diagram.
5. One at a time, tie the rest of the tubes between the tongue depressors. The tubes should be close together but not touching. The raffia should keep them slightly apart.
6. Hold the panpipes with the holes up and blow across each hole. You can make simple music right away.
7. To change the notes a little or to tune the pipes, drip hot wax into them little by little. This will make the notes higher.
8. Each tube will make two notes exactly one octave apart; blow softly for the low one, sharply for the high one.

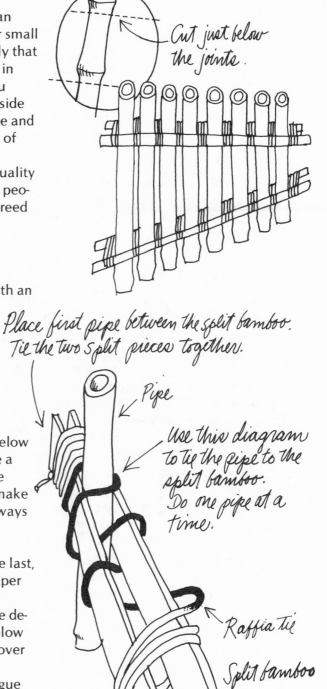

Cut just below the joints.

Place first pipe between the split bamboo. Tie the two split pieces together.

Pipe

Use this diagram to tie the pipe to the split bamboo. Do one pipe at a time.

Raffia Tie

Split bamboo

Wrap raffia around the split bamboo 3 or 4 times before adding the next pipe.

Grass Stars

Grass stars come from Scandinavia, where many years ago they were woven from the last heads of grain in the harvest field. They were kept in each household until the next planting, when the farmers buried them in the fields to ensure a good crop.

Wheat makes especially nice stars, but any grass that carries its grain on a long stem will do. Grass stars require patience and coordination, but the result is worth it.

YOU WILL NEED

15 heads of grain with long stems; wheat or timothy is especially good. (This makes one star point.)
Basin of warm water
Small amount of natural raffia

HERE'S WHAT TO DO

1. Strip away any leaves, leaving the grain attached to its stem.
2. Place the grain and stems in a basin of warm water and leave them until pliable (at least an hour). When the material is ready, the tip should bend without breaking.
3. Using a bit of raffia, tie three stems together near the heads of the grain. Spread out the stems.
4. Insert a fourth and fifth stem from each side in an under-and-over weaving pattern (see the diagram).
5. Bend back the two outermost stems to weave them through, then again bend back the two outermost. Keep the weaving loose. This is not a tight braid.
6. Insert two more stems, one on each side, and continue bending back and weaving the outer two. The braid should grow wider at each bend so you finish with a triangular shape.
7. When you have inserted all 15 grain heads, continue weaving for another 2 inches or so. Then gather half the stems on each side and tie them off with raffia.
8. To make a star, tie four, five, or six plaits together at the grain stems. Mount the star on cardboard or on the wall.

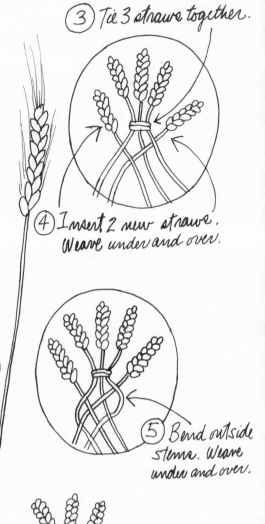

③ Tie 3 straws together.

④ Insert 2 new straws. Weave under and over.

①

⑤ Bend outside stems. Weave under and over.

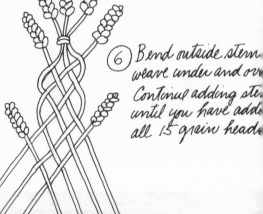

⑥ Bend outside stem weave under and ov Continue adding ste until you have adde all 15 grain heads

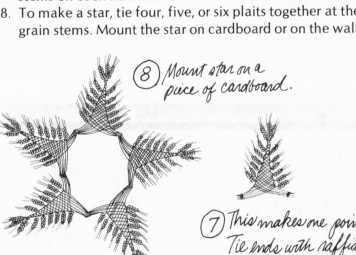

⑧ Mount star on a piece of cardboard.

⑦ This makes one point of a star. Tie ends with raffia.

CHAPTER

Anything Grows

Watching plants grow is both instructive and entertaining. You don't need a garden to initiate a plant-growing project, although a few projects listed in Chapter Three have requirements of space and sun that preclude working indoors. Many projects need only the space available on a small table or window sill and a little direct or indirect sunlight.

Since plant growth is determined by the season, some of these projects can only be carried out at a certain time of year. Where that is the case, it is so stated in the project directions. Some projects can be started anytime since they take advantage of indoor heat and light or special conditions that you set up.

Bulbs That Bloom in a Dish

Flower bulbs are actually fat leaves filled with water and nutrients that surround a flower bud that developed during the previous growing season. Bulbs can begin to grow on their own without being planted, as anyone knows who has had onions sprout in the cupboard.

You can force bulbs to bloom in a dish without anything more than a few pebbles and a little water. Special vases that have a little cup at the top that holds the bulb above the water are sold especailly for forcing bulbs. Two kinds of bulbs are best for forcing: (1) some small-flowered narcissus, such as the Chinese sacred lily, and (2) hyacinths. Both must be purchased in fall at a nursery or a garden shop. Narcissus and hyacinths bloom in January or February. It is possible to force autumn crocus (*Colchicum*) to bloom in early fall and jonquils and amaryllis to bloom later in winter and spring. Bulbs are available only at certain times of the year, usually several weeks or months before they are scheduled to bloom.

YOU WILL NEED

Shallow bowl or dish, 6 or 8 inches in diameter
Marbles or pebbles, about ½-inch in diameter to fill the dish
Water
Narcissus or hyacinth bulbs

HERE'S WHAT TO DO

1. Fill the dish or bowl with marbles or pebbles, and add water until the dish is about two-thirds full.
2. On top of the pebbles, place one or more bulbs with the pointed ends up. The water should be just touching the bottom of the bulbs. Push the bulbs down into the pebbles a little, about one-half inch.
3. Place the dish in a dark cupboard or closet where it won't be disturbed for a while.
4. Leave the bulbs in the dark until the leaves grow about an inch above the bulb tip. This will take about a week. Add water occasionally, but don't let the bulb "sit" in the water.
5. Once the leaves are about an inch above the bulb tip, place the dish in a sunny location but not in direct sunlight. Water frequently. The flower will appear quite soon. The flowers will last longer if kept in a cool place at night. Keep out of direct sunlight. Water it until the flowers die and then discard the bulbs.

Plant tip up

Pebbles

Water just touches the bottom of the bulb.

28

Recycled Plants

Many vegetable and fruit scraps and leftover seeds will grow again if treated properly. It's always fun and interesting to watch them grow.

Some vegetable and fruit plants can be decorative over a long period of time. They make inexpensive classroom or indoor plants. Such plants include sweet potato vines, avocado seeds, and pineapple tops. Other plants, such as sprouted white potatoes, are more suitable for short-term experiments.

White Potato in a Box

An interesting experiment with a white potato that has begun to sprout will show that plants seek light. Prepare a shoe box as shown in the diagram, and put the sprouted potato at the dark end. Its sprouts will wiggle through a maze and come out into the light. You need no extra water because the potato carries its own.

YOU WILL NEED

Shoe box with lid
Cardboard
Tape
Scissors or knife
White potato that has begun to sprout

HERE'S WHAT TO DO

1. Following the diagram, tape cardboard baffles inside the shoe box.
2. Cut a ¾-inch hole at one end of the box near a corner.
3. Place the sprouted potato at the other end of the box, and put the lid on.
4. Point the hole in the box toward a window.
5. In a couple of weeks the potato sprouts will poke through the hole and turn green. Open the box. Are they green inside?

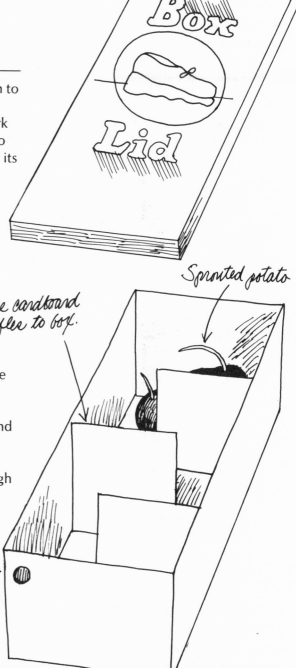

Box Lid

Sprouted potato

Tape cardboard baffles to box.

Cut ¾-inch hole in corner of box. →

A Sweet Potato Vine

Grow a sweet potato in a jar of water near a sunny window, and you can sometimes fill a wall with the resulting vine. Different kinds of potatoes have different foliage. With really good light, the leaves may develop a purple coloring.

YOU WILL NEED

Round toothpicks
Sweet potato
Quart jar
Water

HERE'S WHAT TO DO

1. Choose a place near a window that opens to the south.
2. Poke three or four round toothpicks in a circle about one-third of the way from one end of the sweet potato.
3. Submerge the potato into the jar one-third in and two-thirds out. Fill the jar with water until it just covers the bottom tip of the potato.
4. Keep the water touching the bottom tip until the potato sprouts. The jar will fill up with roots. Continue watering as long as the vine grows out the top. Tie the vine to the wall when it's long enough, keeping it in strong light from a south window.

An Avocado Seed

An avocado seed takes a long time to sprout, and some never do. Try two or three seeds at a time to increase your chances. Once your seed has grown a leaf or two, it can be planted in a pot and kept for years as an indoor plant. Plant up to two or three in a large pot.

YOU WILL NEED

2 or 3 avocado seeds
Pint jar for each seed
Sand to fill the jars, or round toothpicks
Water

HERE'S WHAT TO DO

1. Fill each jar about three-quarters full with sand, and add water until the top of the sand looks wet. If sand is not available, poke three or four round toothpicks in a circle around the fatter end of the seed.

Sweet potato vine

2. Place the wider, flatter end of the avocado seed on the wet sand. If you use toothpicks, place the seed in the mouth of the jar, flat end down. Then fill with water until it just touches the flat end.
3. Place the jars in a well-lighted place but not in direct sunlight. The seeds may take several weeks to sprout. They will first split, then the roots will form, and then a top will grow with the first leaf. If no roots have appeared within four weeks, the seed will probably never sprout.
4. If you want to plant your avocado to keep it permanently, transplant it to a pot that can be kept in a sunny location in- or out-of-doors. The plant should have about three leaves before your transplant it to a pot.

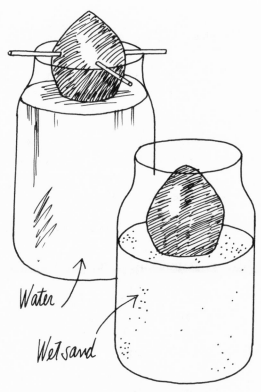

Water

Wet sand

Two ways to sprout avocado seeds

Lentils in Cotton

Using a dish filled with damp cotton, you can get lentils to grow until they flower. Start in early December for a simple holiday decoration.

YOU WILL NEED

Shallow dish
Roll of cotton
Water
Lentils (available at grocery store)

HERE'S WHAT TO DO

1. Line the dish with a layer of cotton, and moisten it with water. The cotton should be very damp but not floating in water.
2. Scatter a thick layer of lentils over the cotton.
3. Cover the lentils with a second layer of cotton.
4. Set the dish aside for a week to ten days until the lentils sprout. Uncover the sprouts.
5. Place the dish in a sunny window and keep the cotton moist. Lentils require several weeks to grow and flower.

Dill in a Dish

A few dill seeds scattered on moist cotton will grow and then can be pinched off a little at a time to flavor salads and other foods. Start a second dish one week after the first to have an ongoing supply. Follow the same directions for growing lentils in cotton, with one exception: in step 3, cover seeds with wax paper instead of cotton.

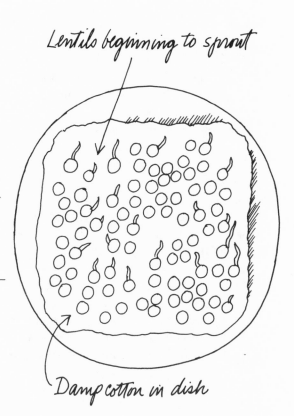

Lentils beginning to sprout

Damp cotton in dish

Gourds *(Lagenaria)*

Growing *Lagenaria* gourds requires space in a sunny garden to accommodate their large vines. *Lagenarias* are night-blooming plants and are fertilized by moths and other night-flying insects, so they grow best during the hottest summer months. Growing *Lagenarias* is therefore a good summer school or home garden project. If you live in a warm-weather climate, you can plant seeds as late as the first week in September.

To save space, grow the vines on a net placed against a south wall. If possible, don't harvest the gourds until the vines are dead. If you must harvest earlier, leave the gourds attached to pieces of the vine until they are fully ripe and very hard-shelled. Then remove them from the vine, and let them dry for a month or two. When dry, the seeds should rattle inside.

Use the gourds for Gourds You Shake in Chapter Two (see page 23), or use them for decoration. There are several shapes, so grow several plants. Two common shapes are a ball with a narrow neck and a ball with a bulging neck.

Plant 3 or 4 seeds at each stake

YOU WILL NEED

Space in sunny garden or against south-facing wall
Lagenaria seeds (packets available in garden stores and
    nurseries)
Trellis of string or net
Rotted bark (optional)

HERE'S WHAT TO DO

1. Prepare the soil. You will need space that allows 2 feet between trellised plants. If the soil is heavy and sticky, add enough rotted bark to make a 3- or 4-inch layer over the soil in the planting area. Mix it in thoroughly.
2. Prepare a trellis against a wall or on a frame of poles. The vines are heavy, so the trellis must be solid with several strings per plant.
3. Plant three or four seeds together; then plant three or four more about 2 feet away. Water thoroughly.
4. Cover the seeds with an inch of rotted bark, and do not water again until they sprout.
5. When seeds have sprouted and have several leaves, pinch out all but the strongest plant in each group.
6. Keep the soil moist as the plants grow, but do not overwater. Water when the top inch of soil dries.
7. Let the vines die and dry before harvesting the gourds. Let the gourds dry a month or so before using them.

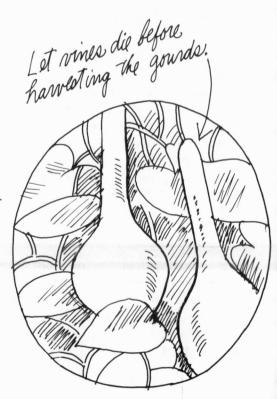

Let vines die before harvesting the gourds.

Signature Pumpkins

Grow pumpkins just as you do *Lagenaria* gourds (see page 32) but do not trellis them. Pumpkins take a lot of space since the fruit is heavy and the vines must trail. Three vines need an area about 5 feet square. They will produce from three to six pumpkins. Pumpkins must be grown during hot summer weather.

There are several kinds of pumpkins, and any kind will do for this project. The kind marked on the seed packet as pie pumpkins or suggested for eating are usually small. The larger kinds sometimes have a jack-o'-lantern pictured on the packet. If you want especially large pumpkins, choose a large-fruited kind and let only one fruit develop by pinching off all but one pumpkin per vine. The young, pinched pumpkins can be eaten like summer squash.

YOU WILL NEED

Space in garden
Hoe
Pumpkin seeds

HERE'S WHAT TO DO

1. Prepare the soil by hoeing in a circle about 3 feet across. The vines will spread far beyond the circle, but you will water in the root area.
2. Plant six to eight pumpkin seeds in a small circle (about 1 foot across) at the center of the prepared soil.
3. When the plants have several leaves, pinch off all but the three strongest leaves on each plant. Water whenever the top inch of soil dries. Let the water run slowly to soak into the soil.
4. Pumpkins, like squash, have different male and female flowers. Sometimes the first female flowers, which are large with a young pumpkin at the base, will bloom before the males, and they will die without producing mature fruit. When the fruit finally begins to grow, leave only one or two pumpkins per plant.
5. When each pumpkin is the size of a softball, write a name across the skin by using a nail to cut through the outer layer. Do not cut too deeply. Let the pumpkins ripen. The name on each pumpkin will form a scar and will grow with the pumpkin. Harvest the pumpkins when the vines die.

A Potful of Herbs

Various aromatic herbs will grow very well in pots. A number of herbs grow long branches that will trail out of a hanging pot. All herbs need strong light or they will grow stringy and eventually die, so find a well-lighted window or a small sunny space out-doors for your plants.

Herbs can't stand intense cold, but since they do like sun you might try growing them outside in the warm seasons and bringing them indoors for the coldest weather.

YOU WILL NEED

Pot with drainage hole (Grow one kind of plant in a 4-inch pot, two kinds in a 6-inch pot, or three or four kinds in an 8-inch pot.)
Commercial potting soil
Herbs
Basin of water
Fertilizer

HERE'S WHAT TO DO

1. Fill the pot to the rim with moistened potting soil. When one-third full, press down gently. Add more soil. When two-thirds full, firm the soil again. Leave the top layer loose until you plant.
2. Plant one or more kinds of herbs in the pot. Here are two lists of herbs with different requirements for sun and water. Don't put plants from Group 1 into pots with plants from Group 2.
3. Set the pot in a basin of water until the soil is soaked. Then drain thoroughly.
4. Place the pot in a well-lighted window. Put it on a saucer or hang it up.
5. Don't pick any of the plant until it has begun to grow well. Since it makes its food from its leaves, the plant must be well-established before it can afford to lose them.
6. Feed the plant with complete fertilizer once a month, and water it when the top inch of soil is dry. Set the pot in water up to its rim for an hour and then let the water drain out.

Mint

This is a good way to water your plants! →

Group 1: Sun and Heat Lovers, Drought Tolerant

Thyme—mother-of-thyme, creeping thyme, carraway thyme
(tiny leaves), variegated thyme, and lemon thyme (yellow;
makes good tea)

Dittany of Crete—gray, furry leaves; good for hanging

Summer Savory

Marjoram or Oregano—stands upright

Sage—stands upright

Rosemary—choose prostrate varieties

Chive—stands upright, grassy look

Basil—green, purple, or small-leafed

Group 2: Moisture Lovers, Need Some Shade

Mint—needs large pot and very moist soil, especially for
large varieties such as spearmint, peppermint, orange
mint, and pineapple sage; for a small-leafed, trailing plant,
try Jewel Mint of Corsica

Ruffled or Italian Parsley, Coriander and Dill—start from
seed

Tarragon—choose the strong-flavored French variety; keep
well watered, in good light; needs at least a 6-inch pot

chives

Oregano

Rosemary

Sage

Parsley

A Landscape in a Basket

Succulents are all those plants that have a reservoir of water in their leaves or stems. The succulents that have prickles are called cacti. Succulents are perfect for a planting project for two reasons. First, succulents will stand a little neglect since they're equipped to live through extended dry periods. Second, they usually root easily from cuttings, so they can be "planted" by just sticking their stems into moist soil. After a while roots will grow, and the plant will continue its life.

In this project, succulents are used to make a landscape in a basket. Only one garden plan is suggested, but each gardener may vary the planting scheme and decorations to suit his or her taste. The plants are sold with roots at nurseries and garden stores, but since they grow so easily, a gardener can also take cuttings from a mature plant.

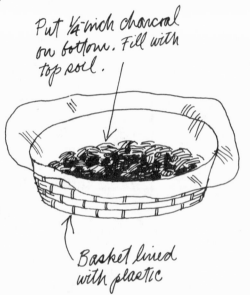

Put ¼-inch charcoal on bottom. Fill with top soil.

Basket lined with plastic

YOU WILL NEED

Wide, shallow basket of any shape
Sheet of plastic cut from a dropcloth
Activated charcoal (available at garden shops)
Commercial potting soil
Water
Decorations: mirror, driftwood, branches, pebbles, small rocks, sand
Succulents: any sedum, crassula, portulacaria, hen-and-chickens (*Echeveria*)
Sharp, pointed knife or scissors

HERE'S WHAT TO DO

1. Line the basket with plastic so that the plastic drapes over the edges. (Later you will trim it.)
2. Fill the bottom of the basket with ¼-inch of activated charcoal granules and smooth it out.
3. Fill the rest of the basket to just below the rim with potting soil. If the soil is very dry, moisten and stir it before using. Don't get it sopping wet, though.
4. You're making a landscape, so the potting soil shouldn't be entirely flat. You can create a mound or a valley, but don't make a mountain. It will fall down. Press gently to firm the landscape.
5. Add decorations. A mirror with its edges covered with soil looks like a pond. Sand and pebbles make a beach. A small piece of branch or driftwood makes a fallen tree, and good-sized smooth rocks look nicely rustic.

6. Plant the succulents. If they have already rooted, take away most of the soil around them, dig a hole, put in the plant, and firm the soil around it. If they're just cut stems, poke a hole with a stick, put in the stem, and firm the soil. A small crassula or jade plant makes a miniature tree. Sedums and hen-and-chickens look like bushes and creeping plants. Remember that the plants will grow, so don't crowd them. Trim the extra plastic with a sharp, pointed knife or scissors.

7. Sprinkle on about ¼ cup of water when the top inch of soil dries out. Be careful not to overwater. Any water that's put in stays in, and a garden that's soggy will eventually die. (Use a sprinkler that's made for dampening clothes before they're ironed.)

8. Keep the garden where it gets a lot of light, but don't put it in direct sunlight or parts of the plants may burn.

A Countryside in a Bottle

Bottle gardens are pretty, and since they are self-watering, they require almost no care. Never leave a bottle garden in direct sunlight, however, or the plants will be cooked within minutes.

Plants used in a bottle garden must like moisture in the air, so tropical plants are the best choices. Grocery stores, garden shops, and nurseries usually stock a good selection of tiny tropical plants. Slow-growing plants are best.

Empty jug-wine bottles or empty bottles from spring-water coolers make excellent terrariums. An empty gallon mayonnaise or pickle jar makes an easily accessible garden site, and these jars are often available free from restaurants or cafeterias that have used the contents. If no lid comes with the jar, use a saucer or cellophane.

YOU WILL NEED

Gallon bottle or jar made of clear glass
Long spoon
Activated charcoal
Commercial potting soil
Stick about 15 inches long
Plants: tiny palm, small-leaf ivy, sansevieria, maidenhair fern, philodendron
Long, stiff wire, such as hanger wire (optional)
Sand
Small sponge
Lid, saucer, or cellophane

Chopsticks are helpful in planting bottle gardens.

1½–2 inches potting soil →

1 inch charcoal

HERE'S WHAT TO DO

1. Wash the bottle or jar thoroughly in clean water. If you need to use soap, rinse it out well. Dry the jar.

2. Cover the bottom of the bottle or jar with 1 inch of charcoal. Don't drop charcoal or potting soil from the top of the jar since it will bounce up and dirty the sides. Lower it gently in several trips with a long spoon. Flatten the charcoal.

3. Add about 1½ to 2 inches of moistened potting soil. To moisten the soil, mix in a small amount of water, stir, and let it stand for an hour.

4. Press the mix down gently with the spoon. Don't pack it tightly.

5. To plant, carefully dig a hole with the end of a stick, set the plant in the hole so that only its roots will be buried, and then scrape the soil over the roots. If you're working with a narrow-necked bottle, gently drop in the plant and negotiate it to the hole with the stick. Use a bent wire to reach the side of the bottle.

6. Plant all your plants. Then carefully add a small amount of sand between the plants, and spread it to cover all of the potting soil.

7. Sprinkle 3 to 4 tablespoons of water into the bottle or jar. Then use a sponge to clean off any bits of dirt on the sides.

8. If you're working with a wide-mouthed jar, you'll need to cover it. Poke holes in the lid if the jar has one. If it doesn't have a lid, set an old saucer on top or use cellophane.

9. Put the bottle or jar where it will get lots of light but not in direct sunlight. Turn it a one-quarter turn every few days or the plants will begin to lean toward the light.

10. As long as the bottle or jar has drops of moisture on the inside you don't need to water. If it seems to be getting dry, add 2 to 3 tablespoons of water. Never put in very much. Too much water will cause the roots to rot.

Plastic sprayers make control of water precise. They can be used to wash off the containers sides and foliage.

A turkey baster makes a good watering tool.

Greenhouse Projects

A greenhouse acts like a bottle garden, conserving moisture and helping to keep the temperature even as seeds grow and cuttings begin to root. A greenhouse with some source of heat to warm the soil allows you to start seeds for a spring garden before the outdoor weather is right for planting.

Most people think of a greenhouse as a building-sized structure enclosed in panes of glass. But a greenhouse can be far simpler, provided it still does its job of controlling both moisture and temperature. The projects below describe two ways to achieve these controls with ordinary and inexpensive materials: by making a greenhouse in a bag or in a flat or box. The Field Notes on Heating a Greenhouse, page 42, describe a few ways to heat the greenhouse.

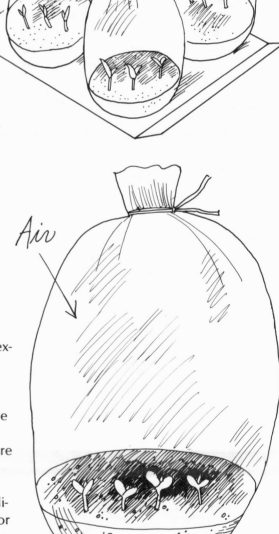

Plastic bags on a cookie sheet

A Greenhouse in a Bag

YOU WILL NEED

Coarse sand, vermiculite, or perlite
Plastic bags, about bread wrapper size (Use clear bread wrappers or vegetable bags.)
Seeds or cuttings
Cookie sheet or tray
Wire plant ties or string

HERE'S WHAT TO DO

1. Moisten and drain the sand. If you can buy vermiculite or perlite at a nursery or garden shop, use it instead of sand. Both hold water well and are lightweight.
2. Fill the bottom of a plastic bag with about 1½ inches of damp sand, vermiculite, or perlite.
3. Plant a few seeds or cuttings. For seeds that benefit from extra greenhouse time, see the companion project, Greenhouse Gardening on page 43.
4. Place the bag on a cookie sheet or tray.
5. Gather the open end together and blow into it to inflate the bag as you would if you were going to pop a paper bag.
6. Hold and twist the open end of the bag; then tie a bit of wire or string around it to hold the air inside.
7. Fill and inflate more bags until the cookie sheet is full.
8. Put the cookie sheet in a warm, well-lighted place out of direct sunlight until the seeds grow two or three real leaves or the cuttings grow a leaf or two. See page 44 for suggestions on transplanting.

Air

Damp sand or perlite

A Flat or Box Greenhouse

YOU WILL NEED

Nursery flat or shallow box
Household bleach solution
Lath (wood strips)
Tacks and glue
Newspaper
Sand, vermiculite, or perlite
Ruler
Seeds or cuttings
Plastic sheeting such as a dropcloth
Masking tape

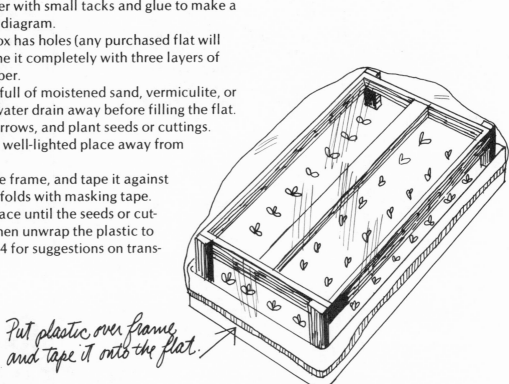

Frame

Glue or nail

← 6-inch piece of lath

Put plastic over frame, and tape it onto the flat.

HERE'S WHAT TO DO

1. Clean the flat or box well. If the flat is made of plastic, pour a solution of 1 cup of household bleach to 1 quart of water in it and rinse well. A wooden flat or box should be scrubbed and allowed to stand in strong sunlight for a few days. Or you can bake it in an oven at 250° for an hour. This sterilizes the box and protects the plants from a fungus attack.

2. Cut four 6-inch pieces of lath. Then cut five more pieces, three as long as the sides of the flat and two as long as the ends. Put them together with small tacks and glue to make a frame as shown in the diagram.

3. If the bottom of the box has holes (any purchased flat will have holes or slots), line it completely with three layers of slightly damp newspaper.

4. Fill the flat two-thirds full of moistened sand, vermiculite, or perlite. Let any extra water drain away before filling the flat.

5. Use a ruler to make furrows, and plant seeds or cuttings.

6. Put the flat in a warm, well-lighted place away from direct sunlight.

7. Put the plastic over the frame, and tape it against the flat and along the folds with masking tape. Leave the plastic in place until the seeds or cuttings begin to grow. Then unwrap the plastic to transplant. See page 44 for suggestions on transplanting.

HEATING A GREENHOUSE

A full-sized greenhouse needs to be heated throughout, either by the sun or by some other heating source. A full-sized greenhouse may also have bottom-heated shelves to keep the soil warm. Warm soil stimulates root growth.

There are several ways to raise the temperature of soil, even when the air surrounding it is cold. In a room with steam or electric heaters that have shelves or covers over them, set the greenhouse box or cookie sheet and bags on top. In a room where the floor is heated by radiant heat, set the greenhouse on the floor. Don't set the greenhouse directly on or next to the source of heat, however, or you'll cook the plants. Insulate the greenhouse from the heat source by placing it on a board or by propping it up on both ends with two objects of the same height.

You can also buy heating coils that are sold at nurseries especially for this purpose. You bury the coils in the flat, and set the plants over them to make the heat more even. Follow the directions that come with the coils. To make the heat more even when using a cookie sheet and bags, place the coil on the cookie sheet and cover it with a layer of dry sand, and then the bags on top of the sand. If you use a box or a flat, put the coil on the newspaper lining and cover it with soil.

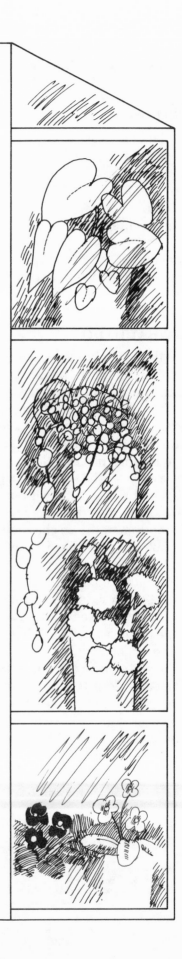

Greenhouse Gardening

A few simple tricks may increase your success with planting seeds and transplanting in a greenhouse. Once you have had success, use the greenhouse for botany experiments. For example, if you plant some seeds in the greenhouse, also set a few identical seeds in a pot outside the greenhouse to see which conditions are best. Grow a pair of small, potted plants, one inside and one outside the greenhouse, and note which grows faster and which takes more water.

Planting

YOU WILL NEED

Seeds
Greenhouse flat or box
Peat pots (optional)

Press ruler into sand for straight rows ¼-inch deep.

Plant seeds ¼-in. apart. Plant different seeds in each row.

HERE'S WHAT TO DO

1. Choose seeds that are hard to start outdoors or that will benefit from extra growing time while the weather outside is still cold. Some seeds that are hard to start without the warmth and humidity of a greenhouse include most herbs such as parsley and thyme. Some plants that need a head start before weather permits them outdoors are tomatoes, peppers, and melons. Start them a month before the soil will be warm enough to allow transplanting outdoors.
2. If you are planting seeds in a bag, first fill the bag with moist vermiculite. Flatten the soil surface, then scatter some seeds a couple of inches apart. After seeding, close the bag.
3. Use a ruler when planting seeds in a flat of sand. Hold the ruler edge down above the moist sand, and push it into the sand about ¼-inch to make a straight planting row. Place a seed every ¼-inch along the row. Plant a different kind of seed in the next row. Plant about four rows in one flat. When you have put in all the seeds, use the ruler to fill in the rows and flatten the sand. Then cover the flat with plastic.
4. Another way to plant is to buy small pots made of compressed peat moss. These peat moss pots will hold two to three seeds. Set the peat pots close together on a layer of damp sand in the greenhouse while the seeds sprout. When the seeds grow, *pinch off* all but the best plant. (Don't *pull out* the extra plants, or you'll disturb the one you want to keep.) Plant the whole peat pot when it's time to transplant. The roots will grow right through the sides of the pot.

Plastic bag

Keep seeds a couple of inches apart.

Press damp vermiculite to firm up soil.

Peat moss pots

Damp sand

Watering

In a heated greenhouse, you can tell that the soil is drying too much when there isn't much moisture condensing on the sides. Since you don't want the sand to dry out too much before you're ready to transplant, you must add water. A plastic bag greenhouse shouldn't take more than 1 tablespoon of water. A box greenhouse may take up to 1 cup. Don't overwater.

Transplanting

Tiny plants need care when they're removed from the warm, moist greenhouse. You'll probably have to transplant them twice—once into a small pot or another bag where they'll grow alone for a while, and then into a permanent pot or a garden.

Use pencil to remove seedling.

YOU WILL NEED

Seedlings
Pencil
Pot (tiny, such as peat pot) or plastic bag containing damp sand
Greenhouse box (optional—use greenhouse bag instead)
Garden spot or permanent pot for plant
Cardboard or shingle as sun guard

HERE'S WHAT TO DO

1. When the seedlings have two or three permanent leaves, you must transplant them. The first pair of leaves out of the ground are not real leaves but are parts of the seed called *cotyledons.* The seedlings must have two or three more leaves after the cotyledons before transplanting.
2. Push a pencil into the sand on one side of the seedling and lift out the plant, holding it very gently by a leaf. It will come up roots and all. If you pull the plant out without the aid of the pencil, you'll break off the roots.
3. Have a tiny pot (about 2 inches across the top) or plastic bag of damp sand ready in which to plant the seedling.
4. Make a pencil hole as long as the young root in the middle of the sand. Drop the root in, and push the sand back with the pencil. Close the bag or cover the pot in the box greenhouse until the plant grows some more. Then open the bag or greenhouse to let the plant get used to the outside air. You can even set it outdoors in a shady spot during the day.
5. When the plant has grown another few leaves, plant it in a garden or in a permanent pot. It's best to plant it in a garden in the evening so that it has time to get used to its new environment before the sun comes out.
6. If the sun is very hot during the day, shade the plant for a few days with a bit of cardboard or a shingle.

Use pencil to make hole

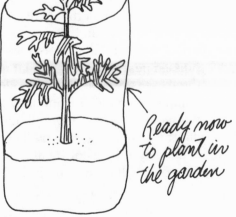

Ready now to plant in the garden

New Plants from Branches

Growing plants from cuttings is interesting and inexpensive. You can get plants for free by requesting a few branch tips from someone else's indoor plant or garden plant. Sometimes you can only acquire a plant you admire by rooting these cuttings because nurseries don't sell the plant, or it has been brought in from another region.

This project concentrates on the plants that will easily root in a glass of water or in a pot of sand.

Rooting cuttings is a good way to demonstrate plant growth. Although most people know that plants need roots, the knowledge itself is an article of faith. They never see the things! Here is an opportunity to see roots grow firsthand.

Cut near a leaf or joint.

Cuttings in Water

YOU WILL NEED

Cuttings of mint, wandering Jew (Zebrina), or willow
Glass or jar of water

HERE'S WHAT TO DO

1. To take cuttings, snip off 3 to 5 inches from the tip of a branch or stem, cutting near a leaf or joint. Remove a leaf or two at and above the cut.
2. Place the bare stem in water, and set the container in a well-lighted place, but not in direct sunlight.
3. Wait a week or two. Check frequently to see the root buds forming and growing out into roots.
4. When the cuttings are well rooted, after three weeks to a month, lift them out and pot them in the ground if they grow outdoors, or in potting soil for indoor plants. Zebrina will grow indefinitely in plain water or in wet sand or pebbles.

Zebrina

Cuttings in Sand

YOU WILL NEED

Cuttings of geraniums (pelargoniums) or succulents
Pot filled with coarse sand (The pot must have a drainage hole.)
Broken pottery (shards)
Pencil

HERE'S WHAT TO DO

1. Take cuttings of 3 to 5 inches long near a leaf or joint. Remove the bottom leaves.
2. Cover the drainage hole in the pot with broken pottery, and fill with coarse sand. Pour in water and let it drain through.
3. Poke a hole in the sand with a pencil and insert an inch of stem. Push the sand back around the stem. You can put several cuttings in the same pot.
4. Place the pot in a shady, protected place away from any direct sunlight. Watch it carefully to make certain that the sand stays moist but not wet. Don't overwater.
5. Once the plants have grown a leaf or two, they have rooted. Push a pencil into the sand on one side of the seedlings. Pull them up slowly and gently, and replant them in 3-inch pots filled with potting soil. Transplant to larger pots when they have grown several more leaves. This time don't pull them out of the soil. Plant them soil and all.

① Remove these leaves before planting in sand.

Put broken pottery over drainage hole.

Punch hole in sand with pencil.

⑤ Cutting has rooted. Time to plant in a larger pot.

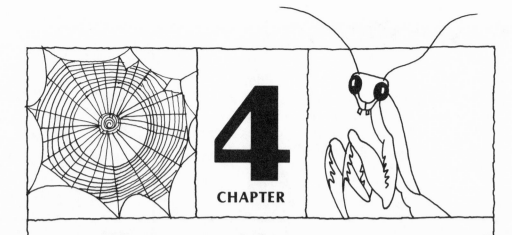

Bugs and Organisms

These projects in Chapter Four will engage any would-be entomologist or zoologist in activities that involve finding, keeping, and examining tiny living things such as insects, pond life, mollusks, and arachnids. Since many of the specimens are quite small, a hand lens (magnifying glass) or a small microscope would make the project more interesting and informative. Observations will be fascinating, however, even without these aids.

Spring is the best season for a number of the projects in this chapter since spring is the time that populations of small creatures are multiplying. If it is impossible to go out into the "field" — a wooded area, a pond, a yard — to collect specimens, some biological supply houses sell such things as water fleas (*Daphnia*), and you can breed your own microscopic life in a jar of water.

Spiderweb Pictures

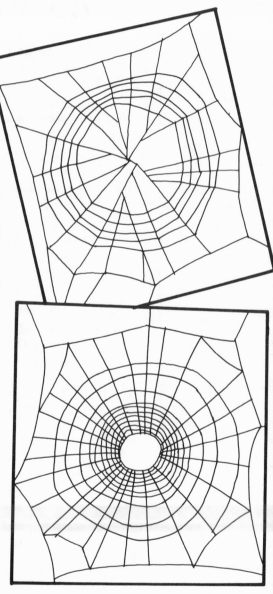

There are many kinds of spiders, and each kind has developed its own system for trapping food. A flat spiral web is one form of trap that belongs to only one group of spiders, the orb spinners. These spirals are beautiful and intricate, and most people automatically think of the orb spinners when they hear the word *spiderweb*.

Each spiral web serves as a trap for only one day or night. It is then eaten and rewoven by the spider for the next night's hunting. The web silk is secreted through the spider's glands. When you collect the web on a piece of kraft paper, as explained below, you don't really bother the spider. It will spin a new web anyway. If you collect several webs, you'll see that each spider has its own pattern and that no two webs are alike.

YOU WILL NEED

Spiral spiderweb
Can of spray paint (any color)
Piece of sturdy paper as large as the web

HERE'S WHAT TO DO

1. Look for webs in the early morning. Look especially in places with tall grasses or plants. Try to find a web that has nothing close behind it. If you find a broken web, come back the next day because spiders try to stay in the same place for their whole lives.
2. Shake the paint can and spray the web with short bursts from a distance of at least 1 foot. Don't use too much paint; it may collect and drip.
3. Hold the paper flat behind the web, and move it toward the web until the paper touches the web. Then pull the paper forward to break the web's anchor strands. The web will stick to the paper and make a pattern.
4. Let the paint dry before you examine the web or try to frame it.
5. If you can, come back when the spider is "at home" and write down what it looks like. Some orb spinners come out during the day, others at night.

An Aphid Colony

Aphids are tiny insects, usually green or black, that suck the juice from plants. The best season to look for aphids is in spring when plants have young, soft shoots and new flower buds. The aphids mass together on the soft twigs. You may also see ants nearby. Ants are attracted to the sweet, sticky honeydew that aphids excrete as they suck juice from plants.

An aphid colony is interesting to examine. Aphids don't move much, and there is ample time to look at them with a magnifying glass. Aphids are parthenogenic, that is, they develop from eggs that are not fertilized. For most of the year, all of the aphids are female, and they continually produce female babies to expand the colony. However, there are periods in which the females produce males. Observe a colony of aphids, and you may see some of the babies being born. You will certainly notice that there are more aphids on the branch after just one day in the classroom or the house.

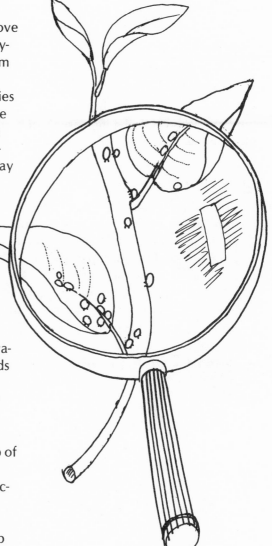

YOU WILL NEED

Branch with aphids (aphids love rose buds)
Container of water
Magnifying glass

HERE'S WHAT TO DO

1. Find a colony of aphids, and cut the branch and put it in water indoors. Don't immerse the branch so far that the aphids are under water.
2. Look at the aphids through a magnifying glass. How many legs do they have? (Insects always have six.) Look for their heads and watch them suck the branch. Watch the tip of their bodies. Every now and again one will push out a drop of honeydew. It's very much like real honey and ants love it.
3. Look at the largest aphids to see if you can find one producing a daughter.
4. Remember how much of the branch is covered by aphids, and then check it again the next day. Are there more? Keep notes on your observations.

Note: Most people mistakenly call all bugs and small shelled crawlers *insects*. In fact, some of these creatures, notably spiders, are not really insects at all by the terms of scientific classification. Use the Diagram of Insects and Arachnids, which you will find on page 87 in the section of Field Charts and Diagrams, to help distinguish insects from other small animals.

Ladybug Predators and Prey

If you have watched an aphid colony for 24 hours, you know that they produce young aphids very quickly. The world would be knee-deep in aphids every spring if something didn't keep their numbers down.

In fact, lots of insects eat aphids, especially certain kinds of beetles, the true bugs, the wingless larvae of lacewing flies, earwigs, and mantises. The ladybug, which is a beetle, is the easiest of these to find.

YOU WILL NEED

Aphid colony on a branch
Predatory insects (ladybug, earwig, or mantis)
Magnifying glass

HERE'S WHAT TO DO

1. Collect a number of predators. Ladybugs may fly away so bring in four or five. One may be hungry enough to stay.
2. Each predator should be handled carefully or you may injure it. Let it crawl onto a slip of paper or a pencil point. Then direct it onto the aphid colony.
3. Watch through the magnifying glass as the predator finds an aphid. Each kind of predator has a different way of eating. A mantis picks up its dinner in its forelimbs, while other beasts just bite.
4. Record your observations.

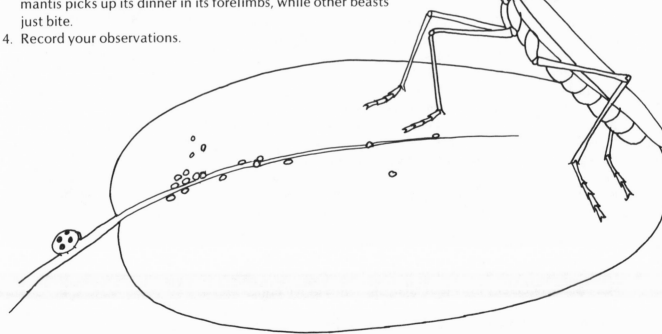

Bugs to Observe in a Jar

Many small animals will live for a while in a jar if they are provided with the proper food and environment. It's much easier to see how animals get through their day if they are close at hand.

Snails are good jar pets. If snails are not available, try a slug. Snails and slugs are mollusks and are related to other mollusks such as oysters and clams. They have to have moisture in the air or they'll shut themselves up and become dormant or die.

Some kinds of spiders can be kept in a jar but not the orb spinners. Orb spinners need room for their webs. Be careful not to collect a shiny black widow spider since it is dangerous to human beings. You can identify a black widow spider by the red hourglass marking on the underside of its abdomen. The best jar spider is a slightly furry house spider. You'll have to obtain a supply of small insects to feed it.

The praying mantis is an animal that can live free in a room. Or you can put it in a very large jar and feed it big insects.

YOU WILL NEED

Small snail, house spider, or praying mantis
Large covered jar with holes punched in the lid or a covered,
    1-gallon aquarium
Food (snails eat fresh greens; spiders eat small, winged insects;
    mantises eat large winged insects)

HERE'S WHAT TO DO

1. Put fresh leaf lettuce in a jar and add a snail or a slug. Notice that the mollusk leaves a thick and sticky trail as it moves. This substance keeps the animal from drying up or hurting itself. It can even crawl over a sharp razor blade. If you change the greens every day, the mollusk may live long enough to lay eggs that look like tiny pearls. Snails and slugs are male and female at the same time, so any of them can lay eggs. But two mollusks will also breed together, so your chances are best if you keep a pair. Depending on the conditions, the eggs may or may not hatch. If the snail or slug stops moving and eating, it's too dry. Sprinkle a tiny amount of water into the jar when adding fresh food.
2. Give a spider a hiding place, such as a ball of paper, within a jar. Feed it live flies and watch. It may prefer dim light.
3. Provide a mantis with a dead branch to climb on, and put in a moth, a beetle, or a butterfly as food. The mantis can see very well with its large eyes. It will grab the insect with its forelimbs and eat it, often head first. How many legs does the mantis have? How many pieces are there to its body? Is it an insect? Check the Diagram of Insects and Arachnids on page 87 in the section of Field Charts and Diagrams.

Woolly Bear to Winged Beauty

Insects are one of the oldest and most numerous forms of life. After millions of years of development, they are so varied that the only resemblance they have to one another is that all the adult forms have three-piece bodies and six legs.

Insects go from birth to adulthood in a variety of ways. Some, such as the aphids, have partly done away with laying eggs; others, such as grasshoppers and earwigs, hatch out of eggs in a form that resembles their parents; and still others, such as ants, bees, and butterflies, undergo a definite four-staged change— egg, larva, pupa, adult—called *metamorphosis*.

It's fairly easy to watch the metamorphosis of butterflies since the caterpillar (larva) can feed itself and the cocoon (pupa) is wrapped in a protective cover. Among bees and ants, the larvae are fed by the adults and the pupae are naked and need to have the protection of adult nurses or of cells in the comb. Among beetles, the larvae and pupae live underground or inside plants for protection. But since a caterpillar lives free, you can watch its life-cycle and then better understand what goes on in the lives of other insects that go through a four-stage metamorphosis.

Caterpillars are a varied lot. On tomato plants you may find a big green hornworm that will turn into a large moth. On milkweed you may turn up the smooth larva of a monarch. Fairly common everywhere are the furry caterpillars that some people call woolly bears.

YOU WILL NEED

Caterpillar
Supply of fresh leaves from the plant on which the caterpillar was found, replenished regularly
Large covered container (such as a restaurant-sized mayonnaise or pickle jar) with holes punched in the lid

HERE'S WHAT TO DO

1. Find a caterpillar and take it along with part of the plant it is eating. It probably won't eat any other kind of plant, so choose a plant that you can pick leaves from every day or so.
2. Make air holes in the container lid. Put the caterpillar and its plant into the container and shut the lid. Add fresh plants regularly.

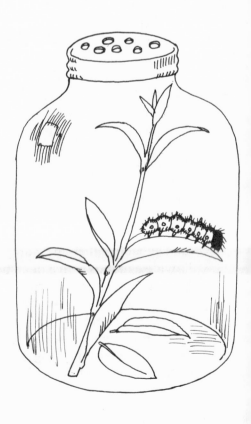

3. Examine the caterpillar. How does it move? The little peglike legs, which are called pseudopods, are not true legs since insects only have six true legs. How does it eat? You'll notice that the chewed places on leaves are somewhat different for each kind of caterpillar.

4. After a while the caterpillar will stop eating and will start making a covering for itself. The covering may be a kind of shell or it may be a silk wrapping. The mulberry caterpillar wraps itself in silk that is often used to weave cloth. Once a caterpillar begins wrapping itself, it does not need food.

5. Leave the wrapped caterpillar in a quiet place out of the sun and watch it daily. In this stage it is called a *pupa,* and inside the cover it is changing its body. At the very end of the process it will be a bundled-up adult.

6. If you're lucky, the pupa will split while you're watching and the adult moth or butterfly will crawl out. Take off the jar cover. The insect will crawl to the top of the jar and sit still while it pumps out its wings and dries them. When the wings are dry and firm, it will fly away.

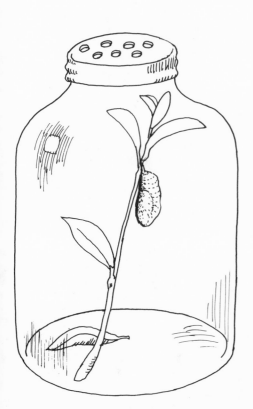

Creatures from a Pond

Many interesting living creatures can be collected from a nearby pond that has fairly clean water. You may find large insect larvae, such as that of the dragonfly, and tiny but visible swimming creatures, such as water fleas (*Daphnia*). The larvae or pupae of mosquitoes can also be found in rain gutters or in a bucket of water that has been standing outdoors for a while.

If there's simply no way to find water creatures in your area you may be able to produce your own. Pet shops and tropical fish stores often sell the eggs of brine shrimp that you can hatch and observe.

Prepare to keep these water creatures by filling an aquarium or large jar with water. Let the water stand for a day or two to age and to reach room temperature. If you plan to collect water fleas, you will need to grow algae several days ahead (see instructions below).

YOU WILL NEED

Aquarium or large jar
Fine nets (available at a pet shop; wide ones are best)
Small collecting jars with watertight lids
Magnifying glass
Jars of green water for water fleas (*Daphnia*) (see below)
Brine shrimp eggs and salt (see below)

HERE'S WHAT TO DO

1. Fill the aquarium with water, and let it stand for a day or two. You can add some sand at the bottom and a few water plants from a pet shop or tropical fish store if you like.
2. Go to a nearby pond, taking nets and jars with lids. Fill the jars with water, and keep them out of the sun.
3. Near the edges of the pond, especially in places with reeds or cattails, sweep the net slowly through the water. Close to the bottom you may find creatures such as dragonfly larvae. Nearer the surface you may catch tiny water fleas. Carefully lift the net and turn it inside out into a jar of water. Don't put too many creatures into one jar. Quickly take anything you catch back to school or back home or the creatures will suffocate from a lack of oxygen in the small jar.
4. Remove the lid and put the jar into the aquarium, immersing it totally under water. Slowly tip the jar to let your creatures go. Pouring the water from above may kill the creatures. If you have caught daphnia, they need green water to eat (see the note following). But beware if you have caught larger creatures, they will eat the daphnia.

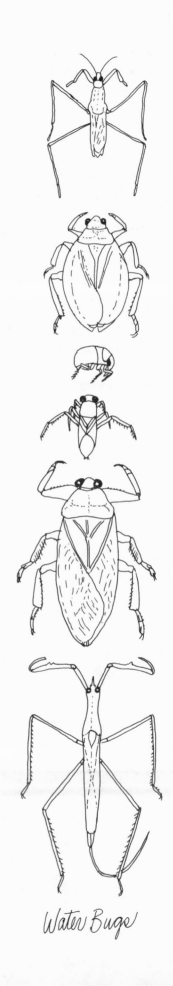

Water Bugs

54

Note: Daphnia eat the algae cells that grow in water; the algae make the water green. Grow algae before you catch the daphnia by filling several jars with water and setting them outside in a sunny place. Don't put on the lids. In a couple of days, the water should start to turn green. You can hurry things along by adding a small piece of lettuce or a drop of liquid plant food. When the algae have had a good start, add some of the green water to your daphnia collection each day.

5. If there is no pond nearby, look for water that has been standing. In standing water you may see tiny wiggling creatures that dive when you touch the water or throw a shadow over it. These are the larvae of flying insects, usually mosquitoes. Take these larvae home to feed to larger water creatures, or to watch, but keep them covered if they are not eaten. They will be flying mosquitoes in a few days.

6. If you cannot find standing water, buy a small container of brine shrimp eggs at a pet shop. Mix salt and water as explained on the egg container and add a few eggs. Keep the whole thing warm and the eggs will hatch. Look at the babies through a magnifying glass. They are tiny pink shrimp. You will not be able to keep them alive for very long, but if you take some out with a net and rinse them in fresh water, small fish or insect larvae will eat them.

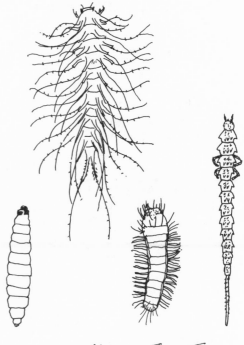

Miscellaneous Insects

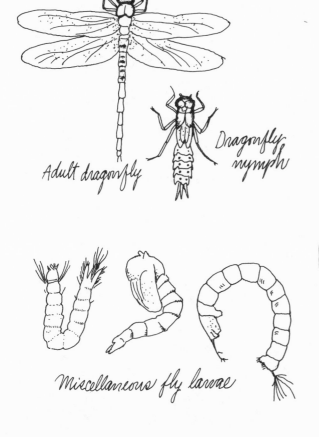

Adult dragonfly

Dragonfly nymph

Miscellaneous fly larvae

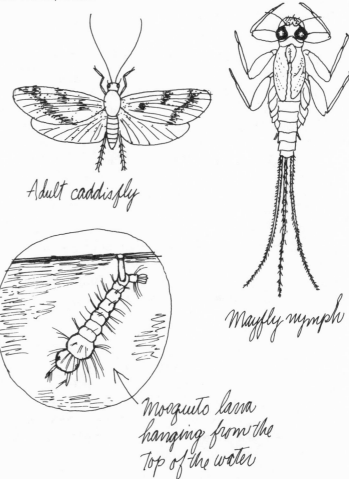

Adult caddisfly

Mayfly nymph

Mosquito larva hanging from the top of the water

Life in a Drop of Water

Even a toy microscope can show many things that can't be seen otherwise. Drops of water from a pond, a puddle, or an ornamental fountain are filled with tiny living things. Once the technique of using a microscope becomes easy, it is possible to examine the microscopic structures of large things to see how they are put together.

For beginners the easiest thing to observe is life in a drop of water. Even an inexpensive microscope will show off a number of creatures among the protozoa, which are the tiniest animals. It is possible to see ciliates such as paramecia, or plantlike flagellates called euglena, or pseudopods such as an amoeba.

YOU WILL NEED

Microscope
Rectangular glass slides
Thin pieces of glass called cover glasses
Eyedropper
Tweezers
Water from a pond, rainbarrel, or puddle

HERE'S WHAT TO DO

1. Make certain that the lenses (the glass of the eyepiece and the bottom of the microscope) are clean. Don't touch them with your fingers.
2. Put the microscope in a well-lighted place if it has a mirror. If it has its own light source, it can be used anywhere.
3. Look through the eyepiece and wiggle the microscope and mirror until the light striking the mirror is very bright.
4. If there is a choice of bottom lenses, beginners should use the lowest magnification.
5. Take a clean, dry slide, and put a single drop of pond water in the middle.
6. Put a clean cover glass over the drop. The drop will flatten out. Hold the glass by the edges or pick it up with tweezers.
7. Place the slide with the water drop under the lens.
8. Turn the focusing knob until you think you see something, then adjust if *very* slowly until you do see something. This takes practice. You may have to adjust the slide as you try to focus the microscope.
9. Once you can see something clearly, you may move the slide a little to change the place you see. Be careful not to move the whole microscope. The illustrations will help you to identify the three main kinds of tiny creatures that you might see: *flagellates, ciliates,* and *pseudopods.*
10. Once you learn to focus on low magnification, try a higher magnification to see more detail.

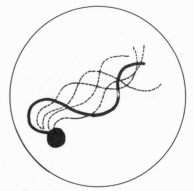

Flagellate. Whip shape sends it spinning through water.

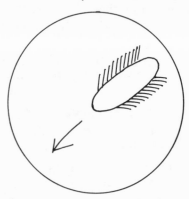

Cilia. The short hairs move like oars of a Roman galley.

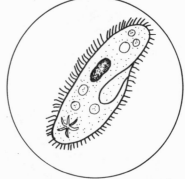

Paramecium (a ciliate)

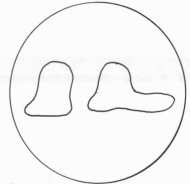

Pseudopod changes its shape as it moves.

CHAPTER 5

Observing Birds

Birds are winged creatures and they can penetrate the barriers of highways, streets, and buildings behind which most of us live. Birds will spend more time in one spot when they are attracted to regular food supplies and nesting sites. An observer will then see many more kinds of birds than just the usual starlings, English sparrows, and pigeons.

Once birds have been attracted to your area, it's time to learn something about them. A great help in identifying birds is a pair of field glasses or binoculars, even the toy kind. Then, to remember which birds have passed through and when, simple records are necessary. There are two pages in the section of Field Charts and Diagrams at the back of the book that will be helpful for birdwatching. A Diagram of Bird Types is on page 88; a form for taking Bird-watching Notes is on page 89.

Remember that once you begin to attract birds with food, especially in winter, you must keep it up. In cold climates, the birds that use a feeder have no other source of food and will starve if they are forgotten. In summer forgetfulness may not do any serious damage, but it takes birds some time to learn where a new food supply is. An empty feeder won't attract much of a crowd.

Bird Prints in Wax

The beach is an ideal place to collect shore bird prints, especially when the tide is going out. Each wave smoothes the sand so that prints are fresh and perfect. However, you can also collect bird prints along the muddy shore of a pond or at the edges of a puddle where songbirds have alighted to drink or bathe.

Preserve bird prints in wax for a study collection or for reproducing the tracks on paper by pressing them gently on an ink pad and walking them across the sheet. Tracked paper makes very distinctive stationery and giftwrap.

YOU WILL NEED

Paraffin wax
Coffee can or old saucepan
Can of jellied alcohol
Small folding stove
Old tablespoon

HERE'S WHAT TO DO

1. Find a place where there are bird prints.
2. Put the wax in the can and melt it over the alcohol stove. Heat the spoon in the wax.
3. Spoon the wax into the bird prints. Do two prints in a row so that you get both feet.
4. When the prints are filled, let them harden. Then pour a blob of wax over each one.
5. Let the blobs harden, and then lift both pieces out of the sand. Be careful at first. They may be a bit soft. They melt easily, so keep them out of direct sunlight and hot places such as a closed car.
6. When the wax is hardened, brush the sand away. In hot weather put the prints in the refrigerator to harden.

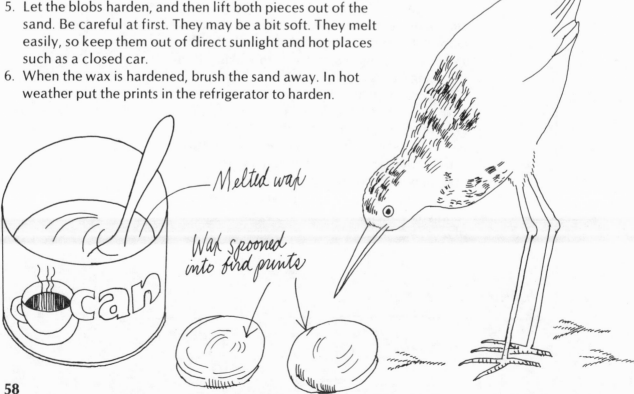

Melted wax

Wax spooned into bird prints

A Hummingbird Bottle

Everyone likes to watch a hummingbird as it hangs on invisible wings near a flower and drinks the nectar. The tiny hummers also eat insects between drinks and so serve a practical gardening function.

Attracting hummers is easy provided that they already live in the vicinity. They love the color red and will dive to inspect even a red bandana, making insulting comments when they find out it's not a flower. The red paper flower that you attach to a feeder you make yourself will attract hummingbirds in a hurry. Once they taste the syrup, they'll be back.

You can buy hummingbird bottles and syrup mix in pet and garden shops. The store-bought syrup often contains red dye, however, which may not be good for hummingbirds. If you buy a feeder, make your own syrup by combining two parts water to one part sugar. The red plastic of the store feeders will attract the birds immediately. So will the red paper flower that you attach to a feeder you make yourself.

YOU WILL NEED

Stopper with metal tube through it (available at pet shops)
Soft drink bottle
1 cup water
½ cup sugar
Red construction paper
Cellophane tape
String

HERE'S WHAT TO DO

1. Buy the stopper at a pet shop. Choose one that fits a soft drink bottle.
2. Boil the water and stir in the sugar until it disappears. Then cool the mixture.
3. Pour the cooled syrup into the bottle and put on the stopper.
4. Cut a flower out of the red construction paper (see the illustration). Make a slit between two of the petals.
5. Place the flower around the neck of the bottle. Overlap the edges of the petals, then tape them together.
6. Find a place to hang the bottle upside down. It may drip some syrup, so hang it over a place that won't be hurt by dripping sugar.
7. To hang the bottle, tie string around the neck and near the bottom. Next tie a long piece of string from the neck loop to the bottom loop on one side of the bottle. Lift it loosely over the top of the bottle, then tie it to the bottom loop and on down to the neck loop on the other side of the bottle.

Soft drink bottle

String

Stopper with metal tube

Overlap cut edges and tape together.

59

Suet Cones

There are two rules for feeding birds in winter. First, start in fall before the birds decide to leave for a warmer climate. Second, and most important, don't stop feeding until late spring when other food is available in your region.

A suet cone is an attractive way to offer birds the fat they need to keep warm and active in cold weather. Suet is beef fat and is available in large quantities at any meat market. You can hang chunks of suet outdoors just as you buy it, using a mesh onion bag, but it's not very attractive to human beings that way. Birds don't really care whether someone takes the time to make a stuffed pinecone, but if you do the result will be less conspicuous and will look more natural in a schoolyard or backyard.

YOU WILL NEED

Large pot of boiling water
1 pound of suet
Knife or spoon
Large pan such as aluminum roasting pan
Wild birdseed mix, enough to fill pan to ¾ full
½ cup sand or bird gravel
Strong cord
2 or 3 large pinecones with open scales
Waxed paper

Mix cooked suet with sand and birdseed

HERE'S WHAT TO DO

1. Fill a large pot half full of water, and bring the water to a boil.
2. Chop the suet into small pieces, and add them to the water. Boil until the suet is melted, take the pot off the heat, and cool the suet until it hardens. Lift out the hard suet and throw the water away.
3. Reheat the suet in the pot, without water, over very low heat so that it doesn't burn or catch fire. (Do not cover the pot. Use baking soda to put out a grease fire, should one occur.) While it heats, fill a large pan about three-quarters full of wild birdseed and sprinkle in ½ cup of sand or bird gravel (gravel aids the birds' digestion).
4. When the suet is melted again, pour it over the birdseed and sand (or gravel) mixture. Stir. Set it aside to cool.
5. While the suet is cooling, tie a length of strong cord or string around the pointed end of each pinecone.

6. When the suet has cooled a bit, stir the mixture of suet and seeds. It will become buttery and spreadable. Use a knife or spoon to pack it into the loose cone scales. Fill the cones completely. Set each one on waxed paper as you finish it. If you make more cones than you can use in your yard, wrap them in waxed paper or aluminum foil to freeze, or give them as gifts.

7. Hang a few cones in the schoolyard or in the backyard. Or hang them out of a high window, under the eaves of a roof, or even on the chimneys of a high city roof. The fat will stain paint and walls, so try to keep suet cones away from anything that might be spoiled. If you have an outdoor area but no tree to hang a cone on, use a clothesline pole, a goal post, or any pole stuck in the ground.

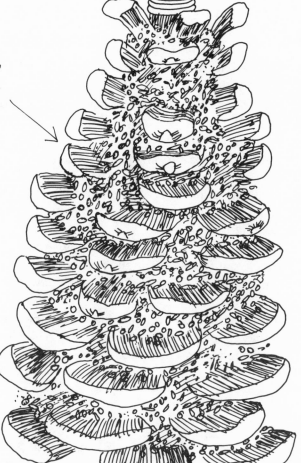

Tie string to pointed end of pinecone.

Force the suet, sand, and birdseed mixture into the pinecone.

A Feeding Station

Summer or winter, you'll have more success in attracting birds if you put out a feeding station that holds plain seeds or suet mixtures; gives the birds a protected place to land; and protects them from cats, squirrels, and bad weather.

A feeder doesn't have to be complicated. The simplest kind is just a flat tray with raised edges to hold the seed inside. But rain and wind *will* spoil or remove the seed from time to time.

A better kind of feeder is one that holds a lot of seed in a closed container or hopper. The seed comes out little by little as the birds eat. With this kind of feeder, it's not necessary to remember to feed the birds daily. You can leave it full when you're off from school on the weekends or if you go away from home for a few days. The birds will have food until you come back.

Many kinds of feeders are sold in stores, either as kits or ready to be used. This project provides directions for a feeder that can be made of easily available parts. Whatever you use for a feeder, there are some things to keep in mind:

- Any feeder must be easy to fill, or it may be neglected. Put it in a place where it can be reached easily for refilling and where you can see the birds feeding.

- Don't make too big a feeder. Water may get in and soak the seed, causing it to spoil. Not only will the seed be wasted, but the birds may be poisoned.

- Keep the feeder where cats and squirrels can't get at it. If it's on a pole in a yard, make a collar of wire mesh around the pole halfway up so that cats can't climb to the top. If you hang it, keep it away from branches and wires that squirrels can use as "highways."

- Consider the weather. If wind and rain blow in from the south or west, put the feeder on the north or east side of the building. Or protect the feeder on the south or west side with a windbreak board.

- Consider the traffic. Don't put a feeder in a place where there is always a lot of noise and movement. The birds will be too frightened to find the food.

Wire the 2 pie pans together.

YOU WILL NEED

1-pound coffee can with plastic lid
Can opener
Tin snips
2 metal pie plates (8-inch; not foil)
Bendable wire
Pliers
Scrap board
Hammer
Large nail
Birdseed
Paint (outdoor latex is best)

HERE'S WHAT TO DO

1. Cut out both ends of the coffee can with a can opener.
2. At one end of the can, use tin snips to cut four holes along the edge, each ½-inch across and ½-inch up the can. Space them evenly around the can (see the illustration).
3. Have someone help you to hold the edge of a pie plate against a piece of scrap board and to drive a nail through the edge to make a hole. Make three holes in each pie plate, spaced out evenly.
4. Make a nail hole in the middle of one of the pie plates. Shove the end of an 18-inch piece of wire up through the middle hole and wind it around a nail on the other side. You can now pick up the pie plate by the wire.
5. Put the coffee can with the cutouts at the bottom into the other pie plate.
6. Fill the can with birdseed and put on the plastic lid. Some seed will leak out into the bottom pan.
7. Put the wired pie plate on top of the can like a lid.
8. Line up the three holes in the top and bottom pie plates, and tie them together with three pieces of wire. Don't wind the ends of the wire too much because you'll want to take them off again to refill the can.
9. Hang the feeder outdoors or just set it on a window sill.
10. To make the feeder prettier, paint it with dark-colored outdoor latex paint (the kind that you can clean up with water). Do the painting the day before you fill it with birdseed.

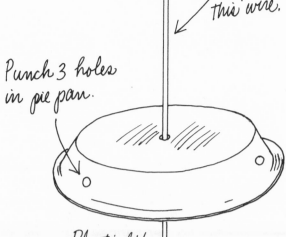

Hang by this wire.

Punch 3 holes in pie pan.

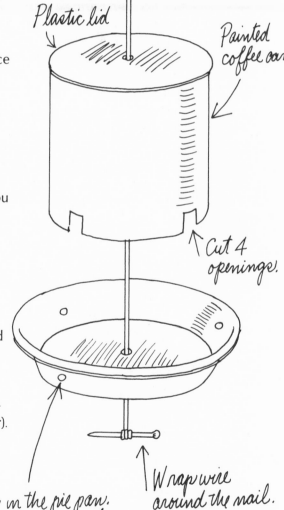

Plastic lid

Painted coffee can

Cut 4 openings.

Wrap wire around the nail.

Punch 3 holes in the pie pan. Be sure the holes line up with the holes in the top pan.

PROVIDING NESTING MATERIALS

You can set out a supply of nesting materials in early spring whether you have a nesting box or not. Nest materials should be placed in a protected spot so that the rain won't douse them and the wind won't blow them away. Use a container such as a large coffee can with a hole cut in its plastic lid. Set it on a window ledge or tack it to a post. Place a selection of the items listed below inside the can. Make certain that the thread, yarn, and string are cut in pieces no longer than 4 inches. If the pieces are longer, the birds may tangle themselves in them.

Excelsior
Straw
Lichen
Shredded paper
Scraps of cloth (strips)
Cotton
String
Yarn
Thread
Unraveled rope
Feathers
Dog hair (available at dog grooming stores)

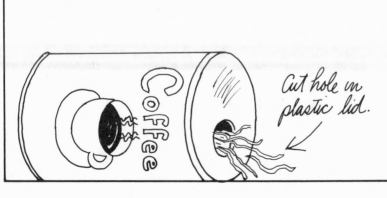

Cut hole in plastic lid.

A Nesting Box

A nesting box or a birdhouse always provides fascinating activity. A nesting place, however, is much more likely to be a disappointment than a feeding station. Birds require food during all seasons, and birds that are simply passing through an area may settle down for a snack. But the same bird will nest only once a year, and it may be very choosy about where the nest sits, how big it is, how close it is to traffic, and how often bothersome human beings peer at it. Even so, a nest box may attract tenants. If it does, you may be able to see the parents feeding the young and teaching them to fly.

Birds are choosy, and their reasoning is not always what human beings expect. The most scientifically designed birdhouse may stand empty while a mating pair nests in a crevice at eye level beside a busy street. There are, however, some bird-preferred standards to follow:

- The size of the entrance hole must be exact.
  An oversized hole admits larger birds and predators, so the bird you are trying to attract may avoid it.
- The dimensions of the box must be fairly exact.
- The area in which the nest stands should provide the right food for the bird you are trying to attract.

The easiest small bird to attract with a nest box is the house wren. House wrens turn up in town or countryside; accept nesting places most other birds would scorn; and find their insect food in many places, although they prefer a bushy or brushy feeding area near the nest.

YOU WILL NEED

¼-inch plywood (3 feet by 9 inches) cut into 6 pieces:
    2 pieces 6 × 9 (sides)
    1 piece 4 × 6 (bottom)
    1 piece 5 × 8 (top)
    1 piece 4 × 8 (front)
    1 piece 4 × 9 (back)
Yardstick
Pencil
Hand or electric drill and ¼-inch and 1⅛-inch drill bits
Small galvanized nails (shingle nails)
Hammer
White glue
4 screws, about ½-inch long
Screwdriver
2 by 4 inch post, 6 to 7 feet long
Shovel
Dark wood stain (optional)

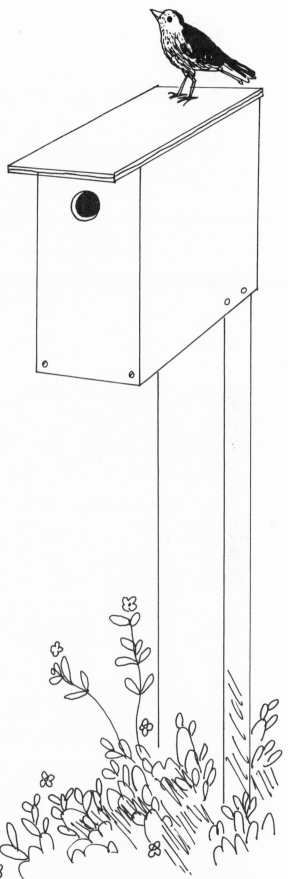

HERE'S WHAT TO DO

1. Use the drill and the ¼-inch drill bit to make four holes in the bottom. These holes will allow for drainage for any water that gets in. Use the 1⅛-inch bit to make an entrance hole in the front (see the illustration).
2. Hammer three nails into the two side pieces and the back as shown in the illustration. Stop when the points come through.
3. Use glue and nails to attach the sides and back to the bottom as shown.
4. Use glue and nails to attach the top as shown.
5. Screw on the front as shown. Screws will allow you to remove the front piece each year to clean the box.
6. Set the nest in place by late winter, before the birds have started nesting elsewhere. Find a place that has shade for at least half the day in spring. Dig a hole 18 inches deep in the ground and set the post in it. Turn the nest box so that the entrance is away from the worst winds.

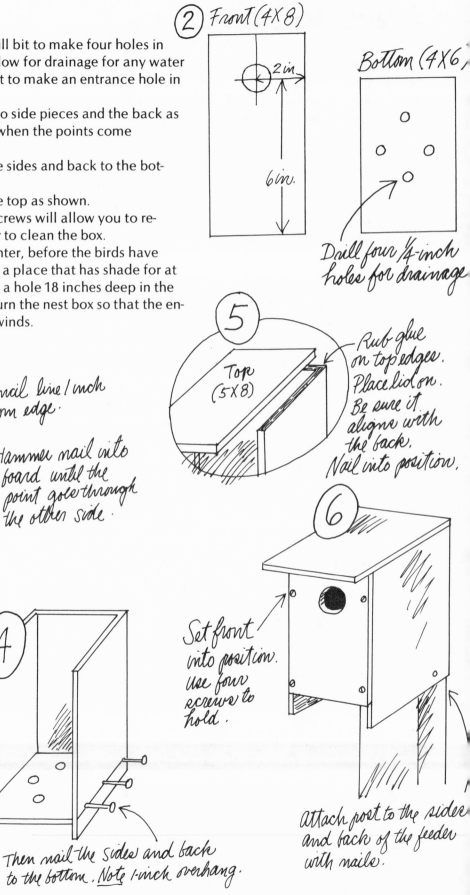

② Front (4 X 8)

2 in

6 in.

Bottom (4 X 6)

Drill four ¼-inch holes for drainage

③ Side (6 X 9)

Side (6 X 9)

Back (4 X 8)

Pencil line 1 inch from edge.

Hammer nail into board until the point goes through the other side.

⑤ Top (5 X 8)

Rub glue on top edges. Place lid on. Be sure it aligns with the back. Nail into position.

⑥ Set front into position. Use four screws to hold.

Attach post to the sides and back of the feeder with nails.

④ Rub glue on three sides of the bottom piece.

Then nail the sides and back to the bottom. Note 1-inch overhang.

Animals

Keeping small animals for observation is not quite the same thing as keeping a pet. Except for the discussion on hatching eggs and raising chicks that follows, the small animals in this chapter are wild (a lizard, a frog, and so forth). You can keep these wild animals, feed them, and watch how they live for short periods of time without hurting them. But you should begin with the understanding that you're going to let them go once you've learned from them. That means that you should collect the animals near where you live, then release them where you found them after a week or a month of observation. The one exception is cold-water fish. You may be able to keep a small aquarium with two or three small fish and a few plants indefinitely, provided that you feed the fish properly and that you clean and aerate the water.

Remember that dirt is the chief cause of illness or damage to a small wild creature. Keeping an animal for observation is work. Someone has to keep its container absolutely clean at all times by removing waste and leftover food, cleaning the water, and so forth.

As with other projects in this book, there's more to learn by keeping careful records. Animal keepers should keep a log in a notebook and write in everything that is done for the animal as well as everything the animal does.

Plaster Paw Prints

One way to learn about animals is to look for signs of them. Paw prints copied in plaster of paris make an interesting collection, and there are books that can help identify the kind of animal that left the prints. Look for a patch of soft, muddy ground on a morning after a rainstorm. In cities and towns, most prints will be those of dogs, cats, and common birds, but there are always surprises. In large cities there are often rodent tracks, and in towns the tracks of opossum, raccoon, squirrel, and rabbit may turn up.

It's tricky to mix plaster of paris so that it pours easily but doesn't take too long to dry. Before going out to find tracks, practice mixing small batches of plaster and making molds in a box of wet sand. The plaster should pour like very thick cream.

YOU WILL NEED

Plaster of paris
Water
Empty milk carton
Stick or spoon for stirring

HERE'S WHAT TO DO

1. Find a set of tracks.
2. Put some plaster in the carton. Add water slowly, stirring all the time, until the plaster is like very thick cream.
3. Pour the plaster slowly into the tracks. Don't dump it in or you may get air bubbles at the bottom. Pour enough to fill the tracks and to spread into a little circle on top of the tracks.
4. Rinse out the carton and clean the stirrer so that it will be ready for the next time.
5. When the plaster is hard, lift it up. It takes a while for plaster to harden, especially for deep prints. You'll have a better idea of how long to wait if you have done some experiments with the plaster before finding tracks.
6. Leave the track to finish hardening overnight. Then rub or brush off any mud or debris. Add the prints to an animal collection, or use them as paperweights.

Stir water into plaster.

Egg Hatchery

Hatching a few eggs is fascinating, but the first step may be difficult: You need a fertilized egg. Fertilized eggs can still be found at a small roadside farm or perhaps a family's backyard chicken coop. If there is a hatchery nearby, it may be able to supply a few eggs. There are also firms that specialize in supplying materials for school science projects and one of these firms may have fertilized eggs in the spring. If these sources fail, post a notice on the bulletin board of a feed and fuel store or a large pet shop. People still keep a few bantams, even in town, and they may be willing to part with the eggs. Get at least six eggs since they won't all hatch. It also enhances the experiment to open a few eggs in the early stages of development. You don't have to have chicken eggs, of course. You may find duck or goose eggs somewhere. They will need about the same care.

Once you have a source of eggs, build or buy an incubator. This project describes a simple incubator that you can make yourself.

The Incubator

The principle involved in building a simple incubator is to warm a box to an even temperature of about 101°F to 103°F and to keep it at that temperature for three to four weeks, depending on the kind of egg you have. A chicken egg takes 21 days to hatch, a duck egg 28.

YOU WILL NEED

Light socket with switch
Insulated wire, 3 to 4 feet
Pliers
Plug
Sturdy box with lid (about shoe box size)
Light bulb (7½ to 15 watts)
Electrical tape
Thermometer
Small dish of warm water
Living eggs
Pencil

HERE'S WHAT TO DO

1. Connect the light socket to the insulated wire using a pair of pliers, and put the plug at the other end. Use 3 to 4 feet of wire, enough to reach an electrical outlet when the socket end is in the box on a table.

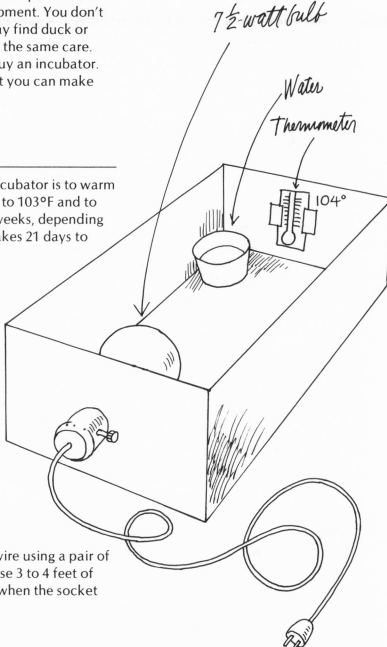

7½-watt bulb

Water

Thermometer

104°

2. Cut a round hole in one end of the box as near the center of one side as possible. The hole should be the size of the socket or a trifle smaller so that it will fit tightly when you push the socket into the hole.

3. Put the socket into the hole up to the switch. Turn the switch on. Tape the socket tightly in place with electrical tape.

4. Put a 7½-watt bulb in the socket. The bulb must not touch the box anywhere. Tape it more firmly if it does.

5. Tape a thermometer at the other end of the box so that you can see it easily when the lid is off.

6. Close the lid and plug in the light bulb. Leave the whole apparatus in a sheltered spot out of drafts. In an hour, open the lid. The thermometer should read about 102°F. If it's much too low, try a 15-watt bulb and check the temperature in an hour. If it's only a little low, move the box to a warmer room and check it in an hour. If it's a little too high, cut a small hole (½-inch) in the side of the box away from the light bulb. If the temperature is much too high, you'll need to use a larger box.

7. When you think the temperature is right, leave the box for 24 hours, checking it every few hours, especially at the hottest and coldest parts of the day. The temperature should never go below 100°F or go above 104°F. Move the box to a room that has a more even temperature if either of these conditions is not met.

8. When you know that the temperature stays close to 102°F most of the time, place the fertilized eggs in the box at least 2 inches away from the light bulb. Make a small pencil mark on the top side of each egg. Add a small shallow dish filled with warm water. Without this added humidity, the eggs will dehydrate and die. Ordinarily, the hen supplies humidity from her body.

Egg Care

Once you have built or bought an incubator and have added several fertilized eggs, you will have to care for them as a hen would. The care is simple. The main thing to remember is to be regular and not to touch or jostle the eggs more than necessary.

YOU WILL NEED

Incubator
Living eggs
Small dish of warm water
Time chart

Make a small mark on the top side of each egg.

HERE'S WHAT TO DO

1. Place the eggs in the incubator with a dish of warm water and close the lid. Make a small pencil mark on the top side of each egg. Do not seal the lid with tape because the eggs are alive and they need to breathe. Leave the eggs for 24 to 48 hours without opening the box.

2. At the end of 24 to 48 hours, the eggs will have warmed and the embryo chicks will be growing. At the end of this period, open the box, unplug the light, and turn each egg over. The pencil mark will go from top to bottom. Add warm water to the dish if too much has evaporated. Close the box and plug in the bulb. It's a good idea to keep a time chart on which you log when you turn the eggs and also to keep track of the incubation period.

3. Every day after that, turn the eggs twice, once in the morning and once in the evening. Don't hurry this process. After the first week, the eggs like a 20-minute cooling period corresponding to the time the hen would ordinarily leave her nest to feed. If this is a school project, arrange to have someone—perhaps a janitor or security guard—let an appointed person into the classroom on the weekends to turn the eggs. Add warm water whenever it has evaporated. Do not handle the eggs more than necessary. It's a good idea to wash your hands before touching them since the oil from your fingers may block the pores in the shells. The chicks are breathing through the shells.

4. In seven days, candle the eggs (see the instructions for candling on page 71). Discard any eggs that are not growing. Open them to see if anything has happened.

5. Continue to turn the eggs twice a day until the last day. The last day for chickens is the twentieth day, for ducks the twenty-seventh. After that day, leave the box closed and the eggs alone until they have all hatched or until 36 hours later. If your room is warm you can cheat a little as the eggs hatch. Occasionally lift the edge of the lid to peek. Don't lift it for more than five or ten minutes.

6. Don't help the chicks to hatch. The struggle is necessary. If the chick can't hatch on its own, it's not strong enough to survive anyway. After you have given the chicks ample time to hatch, throw away shells as well as any eggs that have failed to hatch. You may want to open the unhatched eggs to see if anything has happened. The embryo is probably dead.

Candling

You candle the eggs to make certain that the embryo is alive and growing. At one time people used a candle as a light source, but now the easiest source to use is a bright flashlight.

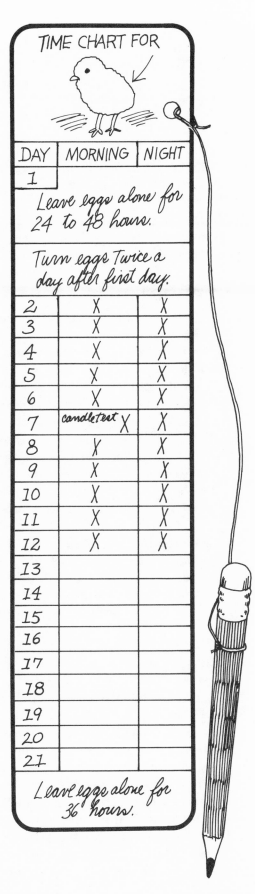

TIME CHART FOR

DAY	MORNING	NIGHT
1	Leave eggs alone for 24 to 48 hours.	
	Turn eggs twice a day after first day.	
2	X	X
3	X	X
4	X	X
5	X	X
6	X	X
7	candle test X	X
8	X	X
9	X	X
10	X	X
11	X	X
12	X	X
13		
14		
15		
16		
17		
18		
19		
20		
21		
	Leave eggs alone for 36 hours.	

You candle eggs on the seventh and fourteenth days, but if you try on the third day, you'll be able to see the first stages of growth. Wash your hands before candling, and don't bump or jostle the eggs.

YOU WILL NEED

Reinforced cardboard (from corrugated box)
Very bright flashlight (three- or four-battery size)
Scissors or knife
Electrical tape
Dark closet
Living eggs

HERE'S WHAT TO DO

1. Cut a circle of cardboard to just cover the light end of the flashlight.
2. Cut or poke a ¼-inch hole in the center of the cardboard circle.
3. Tape the cardboard to the flashlight with electrical tape. Test the flashlight in a dark place to see if light comes through anything but the center hole. Add more tape to cover any leaks. You can check for leakage better if you cover the center hole with your thumb.
4. Take one egg at a time into the dark room, place it on its side on the center hole, and turn on the flashlight. You will see shadows inside the egg. After three days the shadows will look like a large spider; after seven days it will be bigger; and after fourteen days it should fill a lot of the egg. If there is no "spider" after three days, the egg is not fertile. Open it or throw it out. If the shadow is the same at fourteen days as it was at seven, the embryo has died. Discard or open that egg and return the rest to the incubator.

The Brooder

When chicks hatch, they spend many hours breaking out of the shell. You may think that they're having trouble, but they need the time for many reasons, and you must not help. Some may die before they get out because they are feeble or deformed. They will not grow up properly even if you help them out.

While each chick struggles to get out, it shuts the last bit of yolk inside itself. It has been eating the yolk during the time it was in the incubator. The last bit of yolk will keep it nourished for 24 hours. Leave the chick in the incubator for at least 24 hours after hatching. While it's drying out and eating the last of the yolk, make a brooder—a box for the new chicks.

A chick is fragile and needs warmth and care for several

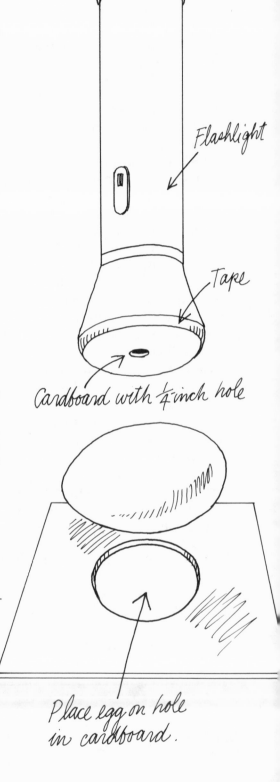

Flashlight

Tape

Cardboard with ¼-inch hole

Place egg on hole in cardboard.

weeks after it has hatched. However, it also needs a lot of air and exercise. Normally it would walk around with its mother, who would warm it occasionally during the day and sit on it all night. After three weeks to a month, the chick grows enough real feathers to keep itself warm. Here is how to care for young chicks from the day they hatch until they're 30 days old. After 30 days they can manage on their own.

YOU WILL NEED

Socket with light bulb (15 or 25 watts) and cord
    from your incubator, or another one you
    make (a ready-made work light on a long cord
    will do very well)
Large, deep carton from a grocery store
Yardstick
Electrical tape
Newspaper
Small, shallow water dish or chick-watering bottle
Chicks
Chick scratch (crushed grain)
Chicken mash
Lettuce or other greens
Chopped, cooked meat or hard-cooked egg yolk

HERE'S WHAT TO DO

1. Hang the 15-watt light bulb in the center of the large carton by taping a yardstick across the top of the box and taping the cord to the yardstick. The light bulb should hang 2 inches from the bottom of the box. Don't remove the box flaps; you'll want to shut them at night. They don't have to be shut tightly because the chicks need a lot of air, but need to avoid drafts.

2. Line the bottom of the box with newspaper. Use three to five layers and change it every day.

3. Set a water dish or a chick-watering bottle in the box. A bottle is better and is available at pet shops. Pet shops sometimes sell just the important part—the gadget that screws onto any jar and fills with a little water when you turn the jar upside down. If you use a dish, use a thick, heavy one that is not too deep since the chicks are small. Change the water often to keep it very clean.

4. When the chicks are dry, put them in the box and turn on the light. If they stay huddled together near the light, they're cold. Put in a 25-watt light bulb. The temperature near the light should be about 90°F. Healthy chicks run around frequently and come to the light to sleep or to warm up. Don't feed chicks for the first 24 hours. They don't need it.

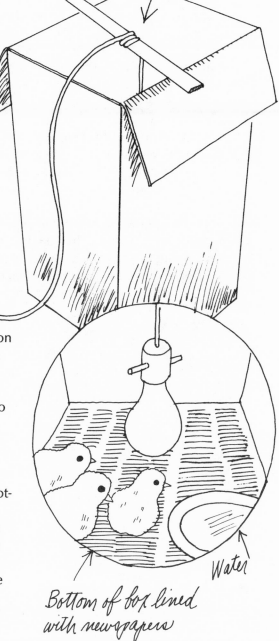

Lightcord taped in position on a yardstick

Water

Bottom of box lined with newspapers

5. When the chicks begin pecking and scratching frequently, scatter a small amount of chick scratch on the newspaper. The chicks will peck it up.

6. After two days, give the chicks a small dish of chick mash twice a day. They should eat it all within ten minutes. Take away what they don't eat. Feed them more if they finish more quickly.

7. After a week, the chicks need more air and exercise during the day. If they can be penned outdoors, let them run for an hour or two at the warmest time of day. Don't leave them until they're chilled. If they start huddling, they should go back to their light bulb.

8. Add greens (lettuce or other greenery) to their food after the first week. They also like very small amounts of chopped, cooked meat or hard-cooked egg yolk.

9. After they are two to three weeks old, the chicks should get as much exercise outdoors as you can give them. They can still catch cold, so let the weather be your guide. On a nice sunny day they can stay out for hours in a place with no wind.

10. When they grow body feathers instead of down (at one month), the chicks can live on their own with no brooder at night unless you live in a very cold climate. They still need shelter, though, and they like a place to perch. Give them a stick or a 2 by 2 inch piece of wood.

A Frog Habitat

There are a variety of frogs, from small tree frogs to large bull-frogs, that do well in captivity. Other amphibians, such as some land-living newts, salamanders, and toads, may also do well in captivity. Remember that all amphibians need a constantly moist skin. Since their lungs are not adequate for all of their breathing, the skin takes in part of their oxygen from the moisture. If you cannot supply moisture because your room is dried out by a heating or cooling system, don't try to keep an amphibian at all, or keep one only for a day or two and then return it to the place where you found it.

You can keep an amphibian in a wire-topped aquarium as you would a lizard, but you should use finer sand, keep it moist, and provide a larger water container. Pond frogs may appreciate a swimming hole. Toads and land-living newts like a moist hole to hide in.

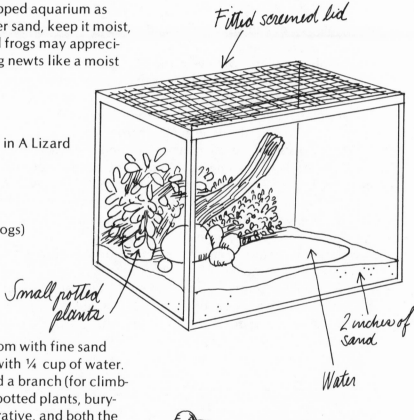

Fitted screened lid

Small potted plants

2 inches of sand

Water

Frog

YOU WILL NEED

Aquarium with screened lid (refer to step 2 in A Lizard
    Vivarium, page 78)
Fine sand
Broken pot or other shelter
Branch (for tree frogs)
Large, shallow water container (for pond frogs)
Small potted plants
Frog, toad, or newt
Frog food (refer to step 2)

HERE'S WHAT TO DO

1. Set up the aquarium and cover the bottom with fine sand about 2 inches deep. Moisten the sand with ¼ cup of water. Put in the water container, a shelter, and a branch (for climbing tree frogs). You may also add small potted plants, burying the pots in the sand. These are decorative, and both the leaves and the moist soil will help humidify the aquarium.
2. Add a frog, a toad, or a newt. Feed frogs with flying insects. The toads or newts will eat mealworms or larvae. Don't overfeed your animals. Clean out dead food and waste every time you notice it.
3. Add a little water to the sand occasionally or add water by watering the plants, but don't put in so much water that it collects on the bottom or it will begin to smell. The aquarium environment should be moist but not wet.
4. Observe your frog regularly. Record its daily routine. Note its food preferences and its physical activity.

A Cold-Water Aquarium

There's something mysterious and attractive about life under water, and even the simplest aquarium lets you peer in to see what's going on.

The bright-colored fishes are tropical or saltwater varieties that require special equipment and expense, but a number of kinds of fish live happily in fresh water at room temperature. Fish-and-game departments sometimes stock artificial and natural ponds with small fish such as perch. Where collecting fish is out of the question, you may be able to obtain two or three fish from this source. Nurseries and fish stores sometimes carry fish for garden ponds. The classic coldwater fish is the goldfish, but gambusia or guppies can live and breed at room temperature and are less sluggish than goldfish.

A number of plants will live without special heat sources. *Elodea canadiensis* is one such plant that fish stores often sell, as is *sagittaria*. Most ponds or slow-running streams grow a little surface plant called duckweed that you can collect also.

The aquarium itself can be anything from a gallon-sized pickle jar to a standard fish tank with lid and light source. Consider shape when choosing a container. The more water surface exposed, the better the tank, since the fish must have oxygen, which enters at the surface, and since waste gases such as carbon dioxide escape there. An aquarium that narrows toward the top should be kept only partially filled so that the water surface is wider. How many fish can you keep? A good rule is one small fish per gallon of water.

The guidelines for feeding depend on the kind of fish. Some, like goldfish, live for years on dried food and algae. Many active fish are carnivorous and will eat such things as daphnia, mosquito larvae, and chopped worm. The pond project on page 54 will provide this sort of food.

YOU WILL NEED

Aquarium (1-gallon to 10-gallon size)
Coarse sand
Bucket
Rocks (optional)
Piece of plastic
Cold-water plants such as elodea, sagittaria, and duckweed
Fish (1 or 2 per gallon, 1-inch to 1½-inches long)
Fish food such as dried food, daphnia, larvae, chopped worm

HERE'S WHAT TO DO

1. Place the aquarium where there is good light but no direct sunlight. Make certain that spilled water will not harm the surface on which you set the aquarium.
2. Wash coarse sand in a bucket. Fill the bottom of the aquarium with 1½ to 2 inches of clean sand. Add rocks if you like, making layers or mounds.
3. Put a piece of plastic over the sand or rocks, and fill the aquarium with water. Then remove the plastic. The plastic helps to keep the sand in place while you add the water.
4. Add the plants. Elodea has no roots so just stick it in the sand in bunches. Duckweed will float. Sagittaria must be planted. Plants look better when planted in clumps.
5. Leave the aquarium and its plants for a week. The plants will begin to grow, and the water will give up any poisonous additives, such as chlorine, and will stabilize. The water may turn gray or green at first, but it should become clear in a week. If it stays green, too much light is hitting the aquarium. Move it to a less sunny location.
6. Add fish and begin feeding them small quantities of food daily, or feed larger quantities and skip some days. The fish should finish what you feed them. If they ignore the food altogether, it's the wrong food. Some fish eat only algae, some prefer meat or live food, and some will take dried food. The main rule is to never overfeed, since leftover dried or dead food will spoil and produce poisonous by-products. It is safe to overfeed living daphnia, however, since the fish will eat them later. Mosquito larvae may become flying, biting insects if you offer too many for the fish to eat immediately.
7. Once a month, take out half of the water and add distilled water or rainwater to fill the tank again. Never put tap water directly into an aquarium with fish in it; keep tap water in a bucket for a full 24 hours before adding it to the aquarium. It may be chlorinated, and chlorine will kill the fish.

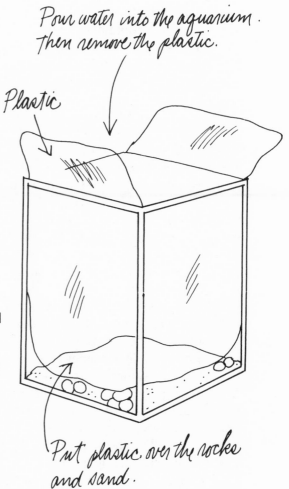

Pour water into the aquarium. Then remove the plastic.

Plastic

Put plastic over the rocks and sand.

A Lizard Vivarium

A vivarium is the dry equivalent of an aquarium. It is simply a container in which you can keep and observe small land animals. The same container can be used to keep a reptile such as a lizard, or an amphibian such as a frog. However, don't try to mix species. Keep each animal separately, or one may become dinner for another. Even if the animals don't eat each other, you'll have problems with environment and feeding.

Lizards require live food, often in the form of flying insects, so you need a good source of flies. You can breed your own flies in warm weather. The most ideal lizards are the fence lizard (also called the bluebelly lizard), which lives in most parts of the country; the horned lizard, which is less widespread; or the skink, which is nice if you can catch one (the young have brilliant turquoise tails). Some large lizards, such as the alligator lizard, will eat other lizards, worms, and so forth. They will also try to nibble on fingers, so you may not want to put your fingers in its vivarium. The only dangerous lizards are the beaded lizard of Mexico or the Gila monster of Arizona. You should only keep the kinds of lizards that live near you so that you can release them if they don't eat or if you run out of food.

Reptiles cannot heat their own bodies. A reptile's normal temperature is a little higher than that of a human being, but it maintains that temperature by sunning itself occasionally and then seeking shelter. To keep a lizard, give it a home where there is sun for part of the day. Also make certain that it has a cool hiding place since too much sun may give it heat stroke, which may kill it. The lizard will only eat (and digest) if it is fairly warm. You should offer water to a lizard, but it may not drink much. Keep the water container clean.

YOU WILL NEED

Frame aquarium or box with one
   glass side, 5- to 10-gallon size
Screening
Wood molding or wooden crate
   slats for lid frame
Tacks
Coarse sand or fine gravel
Cat litter (optional)
Broken flower pot
Piece of branch or bark
Small, shallow water container
Lizard
Lizard food (refer to step 8)

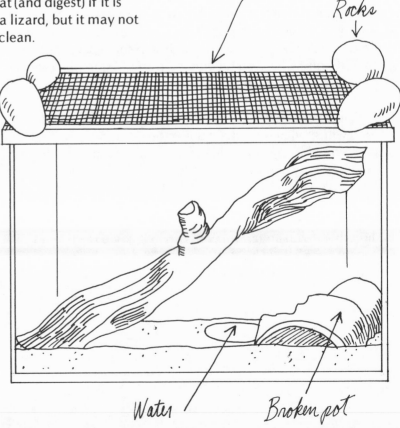

Wire screen

Rocks

Water

Broken pot

HERE'S WHAT TO DO

1. The best vivarium is an old frame aquarium, even if part of the glass is broken. You might try secondhand shops, attics, or flea markets. If part of the glass is missing, pry out the broken pieces and use aquarium sealer, available at pet shops, to glue in a replacement piece of cardboard or thin plywood cut to fit.

2. Make a wooden frame that tightly fits the top of the aquarium. Tack screening such as is used for doors and windows to the frame. Weight the lid down or tape it in place after you have added your occupant. Snakes and lizards escape easily. You don't need much space, so a 5- to 10-gallon aquarium is fine.

3. Fill the bottom of the box or aquarium with coarse sand or fine gravel. You can first put in a ¼-inch layer of deodorizing cat litter and then add 1 or 2 inches of sand or gravel.

4. Add a broken pot or other item that can cover the lizard completely. The lizard will use it for shelter.

5. Add a branch or a piece of bark that is somewhat longer than the aquarium so that it crosses on a diagonal from a top corner to a bottom corner. The lizard will use it for climbing.

6. Put a container of water in one corner. Change the water and clean the container daily. You can partly bury the container in the sand or gravel.

7. Add the lizard and place the aquarium where it will get some sun for part of the day. It is best if the sun strikes only half of the aquarium at a time.

8. Use a wide fish net to catch live flying insects to feed the lizard. Some lizards will also eat live larvae such as beetle grubs, termites, small worms, mealworms, and so forth. Experiment with different types of insects. You can buy or breed mealworms if your lizard likes them. Feed during the warmest part of the day. Clean the aquarium of dead food and waste every time you notice it.

9. If your lizard stops eating or hides more than usual, release it where you found it.

10. Take notes daily and keep records of your lizard: What kind is it? Where did you get it? What, when, and how much does it eat? When and how much does it drink? Does it shed its skin? How long does it take to molt?

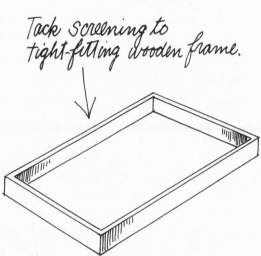

Tack screening to tight-fitting wooden frame.

Horned lizard

Resources

Libraries and bookstores have hundreds of titles dealing with natural history. This resource list comprises primarily books from five nature series. Each series, as described briefly below, covers a broad range of subjects. A bibliography of specific titles in subject categories follows the series descriptions.

NATURE SERIES

The Audubon Field Guide (AFG): New York, Alfred A. Knopf. A good general series for wild flowers, trees, and minerals of various regions of the United States. The book format is narrow to fit a pocket.

Golden Nature Guides (GNG): New York, Golden Press. A series with color illustrations for beginners in almost any subject area.

Nature Study Guild Series (NSG): Berkeley, California. Nature Study Guild. An illustrated set of keys that are far easier for a beginner than the usual key. Titles are limited, including primarily a set of regional tree finders, although there is an eastern flower finder as well as bird and berry books for the Pacific Coast.

The Peterson Field Guide Series (PFG): Boston, Houghton Mifflin. An excellent series with good descriptions and color sections for almost any natural subject.

BOOKS ON BIRDS

The Audubon Society Guides to North American Birds: Eastern Region. Bull, John; and Farrand, John. (AFG) New York: Alfred A. Knopf, 1977.

The Audubon Society Guides to North American Birds: Western Region. Udvardy, Miklos D. F. (AFG) New York: Alfred A. Knopf, 1977.

The Birder's Field Notebook. Drennan, Susan Roney, ed. Garden City, N.Y.: Doubleday, 1979. An interesting book that teaches how to take field notes.

Field Guide to Animal Tracks. Murie, Olaus J. 2nd edition. (PFG) Boston: Houghton Mifflin, 1975. Includes both animal and bird tracks.

A Field Guide to the Birds. Peterson, Roger T. (PFG) Boston: Houghton Mifflin, 1968.

A Field Guide to Western Birds. Peterson, Roger T. (PFG) Boston: Houghton Mifflin, 1961.

BOOKS ON FLOWERS AND TREES

Audubon Field Guide to North American Trees: Eastern Region. Little, Elbert. New York: Alfred A. Knopf, 1977.

Audubon Field Guide to North American Trees: Western Region. Little, Elbert. New York: Alfred A. Knopf, 1977.

Audubon Field Guide to North American Wildflowers: Eastern Region. Niering, William. New York: Alfred A. Knopf, 1979.

Audubon Field Guide to North American Wildflowers: Western Region. Spelenberg, Richard. New York: Alfred A. Knopf, 1979.

A Field Guide to Rocky Mountain Wildflowers. Craighead, John J.; Craighead, Frank, Jr.; and Davis, Ray. Boston: Houghton Mifflin, 1974.

Field Guide to Trees and Shrubs. Petrides, George A. Boston: Houghton Mifflin, 1973.

A Field Guide to Wildflowers of Northeastern and North-Central North America. Peterson, Roger T.; and McKenny, Margaret. (PFG) Boston: Houghton Mifflin, 1977.

Pacific Coast Tree Finder. Watts, Tom. (NSG) Berkeley: Nature Study Guild, 1973.

BOOKS ON ANIMALS

A Field Guide to the Mammals. Burt, William H. 3rd edition. (PFG) Boston: Houghton Mifflin, 1976.

A Field Guide to Reptiles and Amphibians of Eastern and Central North America. Conant, Roger. 2nd edition. (PFG) Boston: Houghton Mifflin, 1975.

A Field Guide to Western Reptiles and Amphibians. Stebbins, Robert C. (PFG) Boston: Houghton Mifflin, 1966.

BOOKS ON INSECTS

Insects. Zim, Herbert S.; and Cottam, Clarence A. (GNG) New York: Golden Press, 1951.

DIAGRAM OF **Flowers**

Parts of a flower

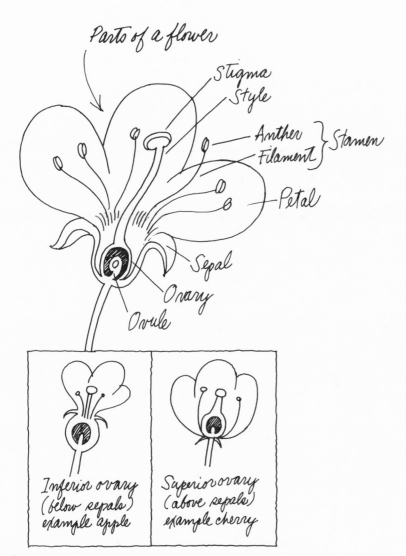

Stigma
Style
Anther
Filament
} Stamen
Petal
Sepal
Ovary
Ovule

Inferior ovary
(below sepals)
example apple

Superior ovary
(above sepals)
example cherry

Composite flower (daisy)

Ray flower

Disc flowers

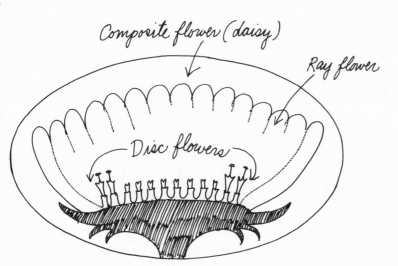

Some types of flower forms

Single	Head
Simple Umbel	Compound Umbel
Spike	Raceme
Panicle	Corymb

DIAGRAM OF **Leaf Types**

Leaves can be identified and described by their shapes, margins, and vein patterns.

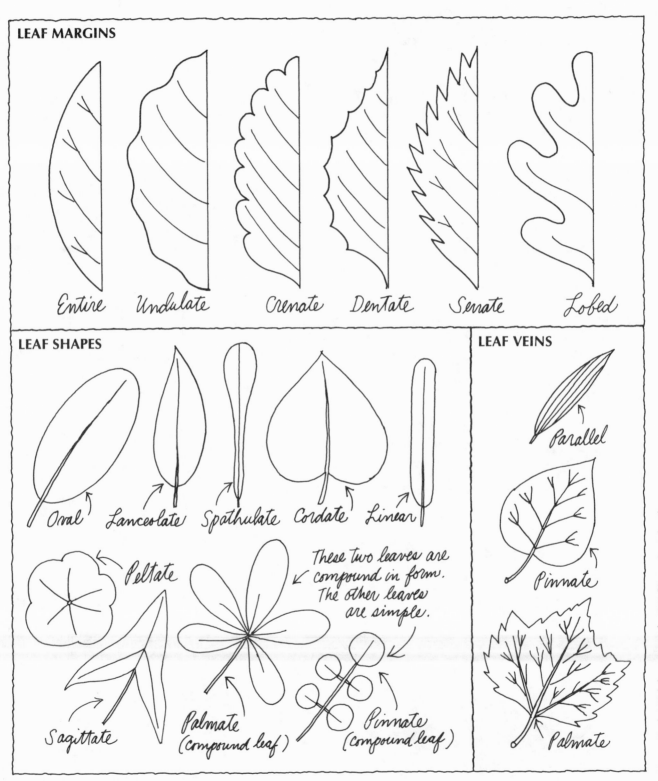

LEAF MARGINS

Entire Undulate Crenate Dentate Serrate Lobed

LEAF SHAPES

Oval Lanceolate Spathulate Cordate Linear

Peltate

These two leaves are compound in form. The other leaves are simple.

Sagittate

Palmate (compound leaf)

Pinnate (compound leaf)

LEAF VEINS

Parallel

Pinnate

Palmate

Plant Collecting Notes

NAME	SCIENTIFIC NAME	DESCRIPTION	PLACE	DATE
Rose	Rosa hybrida	Yellow, very double flower, scented, 3½ inches across	My garden, sunny place near lawn	June 1980

DIAGRAM OF **Fruits and Seeds**

Seeds come in many shapes and sizes, in many forms of *ovaries* or seed cases. Some seeds simply drop to the ground, others are carried away by the wind, and still others are moved off by animals that eat the plants or fruits that contain them.

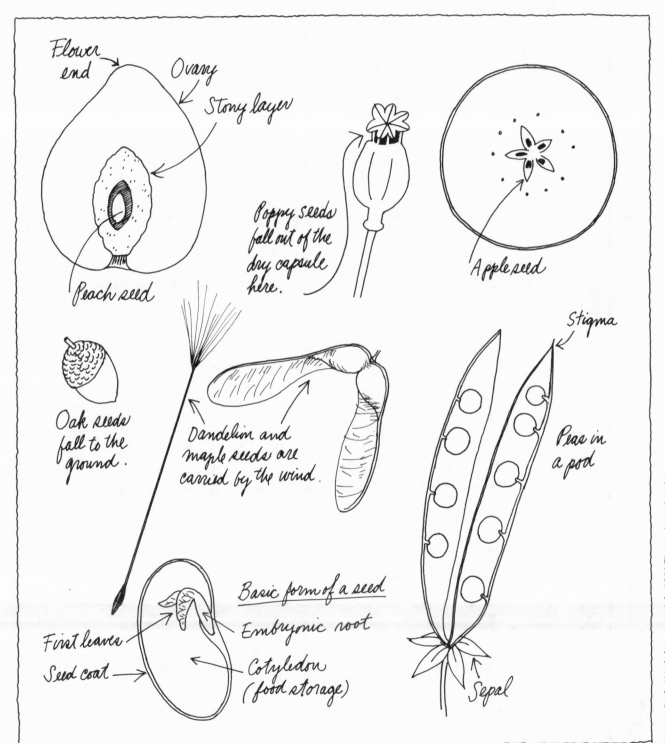

Flower end

Ovary

Stony layer

Peach seed

Poppy seeds fall out of the dry capsule here.

Apple seed

Oak seeds fall to the ground.

Dandelion and maple seeds are carried by the wind.

Stigma

Peas in a pod

Basic form of a seed

First leaves

Seed coat

Embryonic root

Cotyledon (food storage)

Sepal

Nature Crafts Workshop copyright 1981 Pitman Learning, Inc.

DIAGRAM OF **Insects and Arachnids**

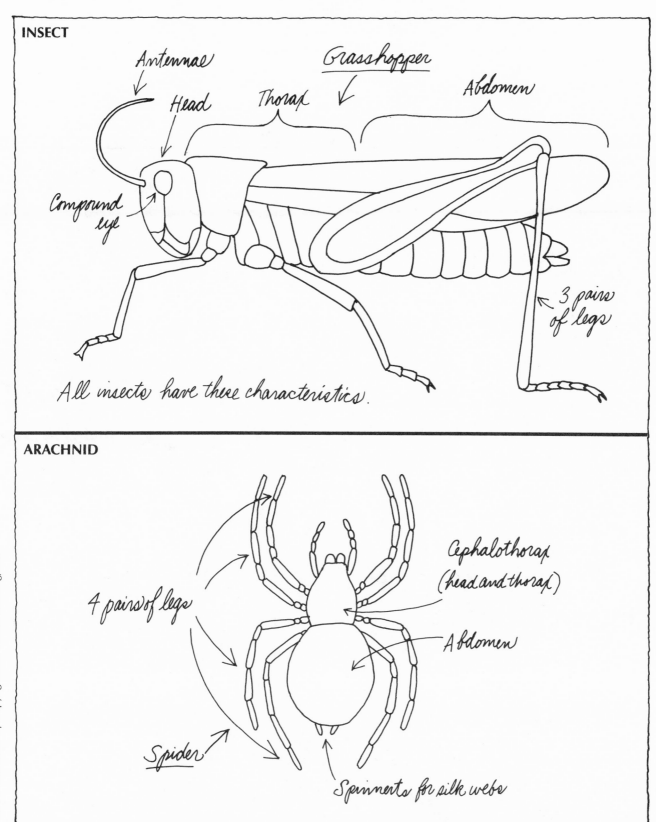

INSECT

Antennae

Grasshopper

Head

Thorax

Abdomen

Compound eye

3 pairs of legs

All insects have these characteristics.

ARACHNID

Cephalothorax (head and thorax)

4 pairs of legs

Abdomen

Spider

Spinnerets for silk webs

Nature Crafts Workshop copyright 1981 Pitman Learning, Inc.

DIAGRAM OF **Bird Types**

Birds can be identified by behavior and shape.

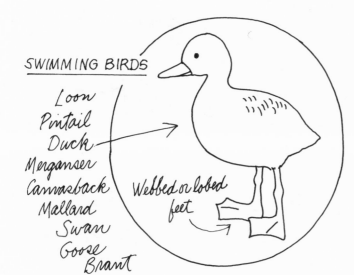

RAPTORS

Vulture
Hawk
Falcon
Kite

Strong hooked beak

Long talons

SWIMMING BIRDS

Loon
Pintail
Duck
Merganser
Canvasback
Mallard
Swan
Goose
Brant

Webbed or lobed feet

PERCHING BIRDS

Thrush
Warbler
Blackbird
Tanager
Oriole
Towhee
Finch
Cardinal
Sparrow
mockingbird
gay

Grasping feet

WADING BIRDS

Stork
Yellow legs
Sandpiper
Curlew
Egret
Heron

Long legs

Flat feet

WALKING BIRDS

Roadrunner
Pheasant
Quail
Whippoorwill

Flat feet

88

Bird Watching Notes

NAME	SCIENTIFIC NAME	DESCRIPTION	PLACE	DATE
Bobwhite	Colinus virginianus	Brown, bottle-shaped bird, walking. Short tail. White throat. Stripe at eye. Heard a double whistle – hoo-bee.	Near Denver in a cut-over field at 10:00 A.M.	July 12, 1980

DIAGRAM OF **Amphibians and Reptiles**

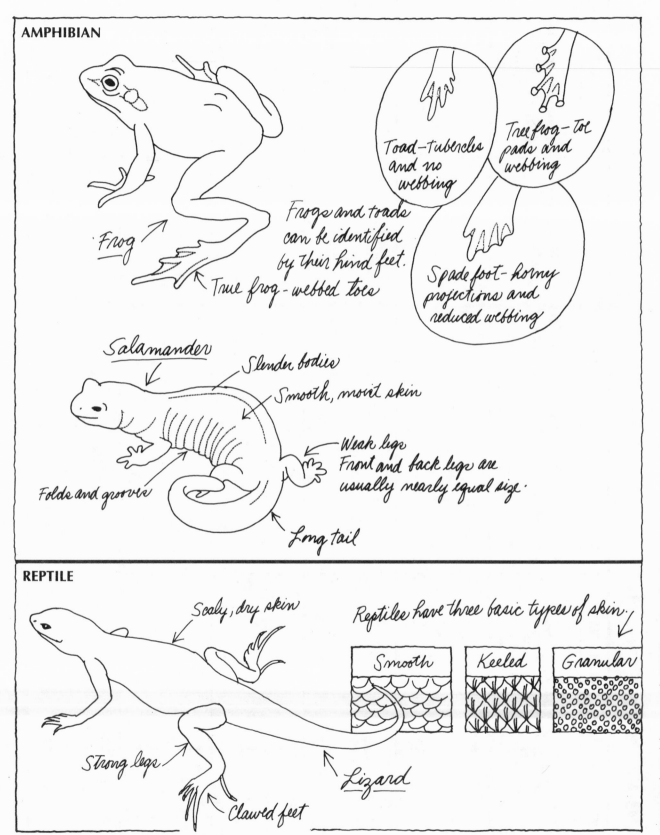

AMPHIBIAN

Toad-tubercles and no webbing

Tree frog-Toe pads and webbing

Spade foot-horny projections and reduced webbing

Frog

Frogs and toads can be identified by their hind feet.

True frog-webbed toes

Salamander

Slender bodies

Smooth, moist skin

Weak legs
Front and back legs are usually nearly equal size.

Folds and grooves

Long tail

REPTILE

Scaly, dry skin

Reptiles have three basic types of skin.

Smooth   Keeled   Granular

Strong legs

Lizard

Clawed feet

Nature Crafts Workshop copyright 1981 Pitman Learning, Inc.